An Amazing
Stones of

Todd Greiner

An Amazing Journey
Stones of Remembrance
All Rights Reserved.
Copyright © 2022 Todd Greiner
v3.0

The opinions expressed in this manuscript are solely the opinions of the author and do not represent the opinions or thoughts of the publisher. The author has represented and warranted full ownership and/or legal right to publish all the materials in this book.

This book may not be reproduced, transmitted, or stored in whole or in part by any means, including graphic, electronic, or mechanical without the express written consent of the publisher except in the case of brief quotations embodied in critical articles and reviews.

Outskirts Press, Inc.
http://www.outskirtspress.com

ISBN: 978-1-9772-4900-5

Cover Photo © 2022 Todd Greiner. All rights reserved - used with permission.

All Scripture quotations are taken from the Zondervan NIV Study Bible Copyright © 1985, 1995, 2002, 2008 by Zondervan The Holy Bible, New International Version® Copyright © 1973, 1978, 1984 by Biblica, Inc.™ And the Holy Bible, New Living Translation, copyright © 1996, 2004, 2015 by Tyndale House Foundation.

Outskirts Press and the "OP" logo are trademarks belonging to Outskirts Press, Inc.

PRINTED IN THE UNITED STATES OF AMERICA

*This book is dedicated to my wife.
Sue is the love of my life, my soul mate, and faithful partner.
Thank you for your love, support, encouragement, and many
hours of editing and great suggestions!*

Table of Contents

Foreword i

Preface vii

1 Set Apart from My Mother's Womb 1

2 Choices have Consequences 5

3 Years of Wandering 10

4 Atheism Was Part of God's Plan 24

5 A New Guy on the Ship 36

6 Who Is the Holy Spirit? 41

7 Beginning Ministry and Marriage 51

8 Radio Waves Now Playing God's Tunes 63

9 The Real Sherlock Holmes 69

10 One God-Encounter Will Change Everything 77

11 For Everything There is a Season 82

12 The Anointing Is for More Than Preaching 87

13 Brought Full-Circle by Divine Appointment 92

14 The Refuge Home 95

15 Expose It! 103

16 Baby Samuel 112

17 The Church Needs a Bus 124

18 Barbara 134

19 Conclusion 142

Foreword

Where This Amazing Journey Started

I know this is unusual—a foreword for a book written by someone who is already departed. I can't think of any better way to do it. This Amazing Journey started with the remarkable transformation that took place in my mom in 1958.

"I have been reminded of your sincere faith, which first lived in your grandmother Lois and in your mother Eunice and, I am persuaded, now lives in you also" (2 Tim. 1:5 NIV).

The above verse was taken from Second Timothy in the Bible. The apostle Paul reminded Timothy that his faith lived first in his grandmother Lois and his mother Eunice. The implication is without question that their faith strongly influenced Timothy with his faith. You know these ladies prayed fervently for Timothy and their prayers were answered when Timothy gave his life to the Lord Jesus Christ. We can never underestimate the power of prayer.

For many years my mother and a small group of her friends prayed fervently for me which led to my personal salvation at the age of twenty-one.

The following is my mom's personal testimony written in her own words. I don't have the date of its writing, but it was written many years before her passing. In the latter years of her life, she searched diligently to find this testimony and couldn't find it. It was amazing how it was uncovered... After my mom departed this life and was taken to heaven, and prior to her funeral service, our family was looking through my mom's personal papers and remarkably we found her testimony. We had her testimony printed in a small pamphlet and handed it out on the day of her memorial service. She entitled it "Now Is Eternity."

Now Is Eternity

Jesus didn't come just to save me from hell and take me to a place called Heaven. He came to take hell out of me and put heaven in me right here on earth.

We sing the song about abiding. There's a lot of difference between abiding and renting a room. If Jesus is living in the guest room, He doesn't own the house. He's not abiding there. If my mother-in-law calls me and says she is coming over to spend the evening with me, that isn't too bad because I can clean up the kitchen, dining room, den, bathroom and living room, but God forbid she's going to abide; otherwise, the whole house is going to have to be overhauled because she's going to be in every room of the house. She is going to LIVE with me. God doesn't want to rent my guest room; He wants to abide with me to make me heavenly on the inside.

When I joined the Methodist Church, the funny thing was, it didn't change me. Being a Methodist didn't change me one bit. The day after I became a Methodist, I still had the same old rotten disposition, same temper, same screaming at my kids and husband. Nothing happened! The Lord let me muddle around in this behavior for seven years.

Because of different sicknesses, the doctors took a lot of things out of me, but God had to put something in me if I was going to be different. John the Baptist makes us better, but Jesus came to transform us.

I had people ask me if I was a Christian and it would make

me furious. I said, "If I wasn't, do you think I'd be going to church?"

One lady said, "Your ego could make you do that." She asked, "If you are a Christian, when did you become a Christian?"

She wanted me to witness. I told her that I did not become a Christian, I was born a Christian. She said, "Honey, you've never read the Bible because it says that you must be re-born. It is not the will of the flesh, and it is not of your mind, but it must be of God."

I kept my distance from people like her. Besides, her self-styled happiness bothered me. I couldn't fight this thing. Everywhere I'd look there it was, only I couldn't see it. I didn't know what I was looking for. I didn't know what I was feeling–only that it was crushing me to death. God was nudging me into a corner and just loving me until I couldn't stand it anymore.

I went to church Sunday after Sunday and nothing happened. Jesus was literally dying to save me, and I wouldn't let Him save me. Well, I didn't know who He was. There was a sign on the highway that almost drove me mad looking at it. It said, "Christ died for the ungodly… And the wages of sin is death." I thought, "Who were those idiots that put that there?" That's terrible, but the sign was saying, "Baby, they're talking about you. You've got a dozen jobs in the church, but you haven't got Jesus Christ in your heart. Oh, you know all about Him, but you don't know Him; you don't know Him at all."

I was hospitalized again, and fearing the verdict was going to be the "Big C" I was just terrified. I was afraid to die but didn't know how to live. Jesus said this is what it is: Not Knowing Him. As I lay there in the hospital bed on that first Friday in November, I stared out the window at the cold rain beating against the glass, then stared at the crucifix hanging on the wall in front of me, my thoughts strayed again to death, God, and eternity – thinking they were all three synonymous.

The doctor came into the room with a look of doom and gloom on his face. He told me he must remove my left lung. He said the hemorrhaging was due to the infection and would spread to the other lung if not removed. Surgery was scheduled for Monday. Because of the mental and physical state that I was in, this seemed a death sentence to me. It didn't matter that thousands of people had surgery more involved than this and lived through it. Putting me under duress, he then released me for the weekend. I did not return Sunday. My husband didn't force me to. He called my medical doctor, and he was told to take me to Barnes. He gave the name of the best specialist there.

A concerned friend asked me if I felt like going to a special meeting at our church on Wednesday evening. The layman was to speak on prayer, but he spoke about Jesus Christ and my desperate need for Jesus Christ. When he spoke of Pontius Pilate asking the crowd what he should do with Jesus because he could find no fault in him, the crowd cried in one accord, "Crucify him! Crucify him!" I saw myself standing there with the crowd and my heart screaming "Crucify him." I knew then that my heart was desperately wicked. The speaker said that one drop of the Divine chemistry of the blood of Jesus Christ could cleanse the whole world (everyone in the world) of their sin. As he closed, he said that God's plan of salvation was not to get me out of hell and get me into heaven but to get hell out of me and get heaven into me right here on earth, and that blew my mind. I never heard such a thing.

You don't have to be at an altar to be saved. You've just got to be desperate in your own heart. You've just got to come to the end of your own rope where there's not even a knot in it, but there is Jesus Christ.

The first thing I asked Jesus was, "What would you have me to do?" I thought because Isaiah asked the same question, that I should also. He said, "What can you do?"

I said, "Nothing."

He said, "That's the most profound statement you have ever made. Stop trying and start trusting. I don't want your service; I want you!"

When you are a baby Christian you don't know any other Christians, that's the nicest time of your life because then you go to God for everything. If you've got somebody to run to and cry on their shoulder and get them to do your praying for you, you're never going to trust God. You're going to trust people to get to God.

At the church that night I gave him my will, and my mind, but it wasn't until the next day that I gave him my heart. The lay speaker had promised that God was going to make me different. I thought in order to make my life different he sure had to change some of my relatives. I thought God was just going to snap a finger and my husband was going to fall at my feet and we would have peace. I thought my sister, who had always argued with me, would admit I was right. I thought my kids would instantly obey and we would have peace, but you know, that isn't His plan of salvation at all. He didn't touch them. He changed me and my attitude toward them.

I don't know if this happens in every Christian's life, but it happened in mine. Jesus asked me to kneel, but I didn't know how to pray. I didn't know what He was going to pull next, so I said with all my heart, "God, be merciful to me a sinner." And he said, "What's the worst sin you have ever committed and call it by its right name."

It was so hard for me to say it out loud to Jesus, but I finally just said it. Now, I didn't feel any club over my head. He said, "What's the next thing, the next thing, the next…?" He took me back to every lie I ever told, every bad thing I'd ever done, and it was an awful, awful, time. I don't ever want to go through a thing like that again. I heard someone say after having gone through an experience like mine, "Oh Lord, I'm not fit to live."

And Jesus said, "Who told you that you have been living? Now I'm going to show you what life is all about. I'm going to send you joy, peace, and love, and you're going to be a joyful person." He just makes a new person.

All God asked me to do now was to provide a heavenly atmosphere in my home because heaven was now in my heart. He didn't want to take me to some faraway place called Heaven, he wanted me to make my home a heaven on earth for my family. Jesus died to keep me from getting mad and throwing things. Without him we're just miserable. All He did was change the inside of me and when He did that, the outside changed. I didn't see any angels or anything like that. The main thing that happened was my reason for living, for Jesus had silently come into my heart when I made it an empty manger instead of the busy inn. The wise men had no preconceived idea of God. They knew who they were looking for. They came to Him, saw Him, recognized Him, worshipped Him and then went home a different way.

When I opened my heart to Him a great peace flooded my soul and it felt like the weight of the world had fallen off me, and wave after wave of His love poured through my entire being. I did not realize until later that day that I'd been healed. I asked the Lord about this. I said, "I didn't even ask you to heal me and yet you did."

He said, "I had to heal the cancer in your soul before healing the cancer in your lung. If you were to gain the whole world of physical health and wealth and lose your soul what have you gained?"

My husband took me to the doctor at Barnes Hospital and he confirmed my healing. It has remained to this day.

Preface

Stones of Remembrance

When all the people had crossed the Jordan, the LORD said to Joshua, "Now choose twelve men, one from each tribe. Tell them, 'Take twelve stones from the very place where the priests are standing in the middle of the Jordan. Carry them out and pile them up at the place where you will camp tonight.'" So Joshua called together the twelve men he had chosen— one from each of the tribes of Israel. He told them, "Go into the middle of the Jordan, in front of the Ark of the LORD your God. Each of you must pick up one stone and carry it out on your shoulder— twelve stones in all, one for each of the twelve tribes of Israel. **We will use these stones to build a memorial. In the future your children will ask you, 'What do these stones mean?'** *Then you can tell them, 'They remind us that the Jordan River stopped flowing when the Ark of the LORD's Covenant went across.'* **These stones will stand as a memorial** *among the people of Israel forever" (Josh. 4:1-7 NLT).*

Crossing the Jordan River was a key event in Israel's history. Just as crossing the Red Sea changed Israel's standing from slavery to freedom, passing through the Jordan into the Promised Land transformed Israel from a wandering horde into an established nation. God did not want His people to forget these incredible events in the history of their nation. The stones were set up as a memorial of remembrance. The significance of this was twofold. First, as a nation, they should never forget what God did for them and second, that the remembrance of these events would be passed down to their children and to their children's children.

I write this book first and foremost to the glory and praise of my Lord and Savior Jesus Christ. Second, this is my memorial built with my stones of remembrance to my children and my children's children.

Every story in this book is a stone cemented as a memorial and I pray that my family and family to come will never forget these great events preserving and encouraging a personal relationship with Jesus Christ. These stories are much more than stones of remembrance. *To me, they are precious stones, jewels, and rubies adorning a beautiful memorial.* I have treasured these events deeply in the core of my soul.

I can't stop thinking about Elihu in the book of Job. He was a young man, waiting and listening to Job's other three friends and felt like he was about to burst if he didn't share his heart…

"For I am full of pent-up words, and the spirit within me urges me on. I am like a cask of wine without a vent, like a new wineskin ready to burst! I must speak to find relief…" (Job 32:18,19 NLT)

The context is different, but the feeling is the same. It's like I can't hold back any longer; I want to shout these stories from the rooftop. I have fought condemnation in wanting to write this book. Even though I felt the leadership and nudging of the Holy Spirit, the enemy fought me in regard to my motives. But this is not a book about personal accomplishments at all! It's a book testifying to the fact that Jesus Christ truly is the same yesterday, today and forever. He still speaks clearly to His people and still works in amazing ways!

"Jesus Christ is the same yesterday, today, and forever." (Heb. 13:8 NLT).

For the last two years I have felt a strong urging of the Holy Spirit to write this book and yet it has been such a struggle. Part of the struggle has been knowing the risk I'm taking sharing these stories. There can be disappointment when you share precious things from your heart, and they're not taken seriously. What finally brought me to the place of knowing for sure that I should write this book was understanding that I write it first and foremost as a testimony to Jesus Christ for His incredible greatness and to the praise of who He is.

This book is being written through a labor of prayer. I pray that every chapter, page, and sentence will be led by the Holy Spirit. Nothing in this book has been exaggerated, inflated, retold or re-fabricated. Every one of them happened.

I pray that this book would be cherished by my family who know me so well. Most of these stories they already know but they also know that I would not write anything that isn't completely true. Last, but not least, I pray this book would be inspiring to those who read it.

Hearing the Voice of God

"Walk with the Wise" has written the following…

"Research reported by the National Science Foundation found that the average person has about 12,000 to 60,000 thoughts per day! Out of those thousands of thoughts, could any of them be God speaking to you? If so, how can you tell? The ability to tell which thoughts are from God and which thoughts are just from yourself will get easier with experience.

You are probably already hearing God in your thoughts but don't even realize it's God speaking through your mind!"

I can attest to the above statement as being true. It's not rocket science, it's called "childlike faith."

This book is a collection of stories of how God spoke to me.

Please listen to what I have to say in this preface before you close the book, set it aside, and quickly conclude that I am scripturally unsound. I have never heard the audible voice of God. I have never seen writing on the wall. I have never been struck by lightning. I simply have heard His voice many times in my mind – spirit – soul - heart. Simply said, He has spoken many times in my thoughts, and I had the simple faith, knowing it was Him. The Holy Spirit is not going to speak to us in some strange way that contradicts what His Word teaches. I am not ignorant of Satan's tricks. Nor am I foolish. There are millions of voices in this world, and we need to walk closely enough with the Lord Jesus Christ to develop the sensitivity and discernment of hearing His voice above all the other voices.

I am so glad that I didn't run to the theological library to research if it was God or not. Had I done that, I would never have obeyed and never experienced these beautiful times with the Holy Spirit.

Please don't misunderstand me. If you have ever listened to one of my teachings, they are consumed with Scripture. I am a strong advocate that the children of God should study the Scriptures thoroughly, making sure we do not misrepresent what the Word teaches. The apostle Paul gave good advice to the Corinthians…

"But I am afraid that, as the serpent deceived Eve by his craftiness, your minds will be led astray from the simplicity and purity of devotion to Christ." (2 Cor. 11:3 NASB).

It is amazing how some Christian leaders will go to great lengths explaining something away that they either don't understand or never personally experienced. Hearing the voice of God falls into that category. I respect caution but, as the saying goes, "Don't throw the baby out with the bathwater."

Anyone can use the Bible to either defend or destroy whatever they wish.

The intention of this book is not for the purpose of theological debate. I am simply sharing stories of how God spoke to me clearly and the proof is seen in the amazing events that followed. I am not trying to prove a point; I am a witness to the fact that Jesus Christ is the same yesterday, today and forever.

Todd

"Therefore, as it is written: *"Let him who boasts boast in the Lord"*

(1 Cor. 1:31).

"But as for me, it is good to be near God. I have made the Sovereign LORD my refuge; *I will tell of all your deeds*" (Ps. 73:28 NIV).

"Sing to him, sing praise to him; *tell of all his wonderful acts*"

(Ps. 105:2).

1

Set Apart from My Mother's Womb

"Before I formed you in the womb, I knew you, before you were born, I set you apart…" (Jer. 1:5 NIV)

In the spring of 1951, my mom found out that she was pregnant. This brought a tremendous amount of stress; my dad was married to another woman. My mom was twenty-five years old and my dad thirty-seven. Only eight months before, my mom had lost her first husband to a heart attack. His name was Charles (Blackie) Kenner. Blackie was one month shy of his 43rd birthday. His untimely death left my mom with a four-year-old daughter, a tavern, and a broken heart.

Blackie had been the owner of "Blackie's Tavern" which now belonged solely to a young woman with a very young child. Like so many other young women, my mom was left with a void in her heart and needed something or someone to fill that void. My dad had known my mom since he often visited the tavern. Emptiness in the heart will often leave a person vulnerable. Blackie had been nineteen years older than mom; dad was thirteen years older.

Many women who do not have a godly father figure in their family lack good judgment when they get older in choosing a marriage partner. Mom grew up in an impoverished family (being poor is not a weakness). She had a godly mother but an alcoholic father. Spending quality time with your father was something unheard of in her childhood.

Was it her lack of having a healthy home environment with a godly father that led her to relationships with older men? Many experts would say yes.

When mom found out that she was pregnant, instead of excitement; there were feelings of denial, grief, worry, and fear. These feelings led to a decision that she would significantly regret.

In 1951 abortion statistics were entirely different than modern day statistics. In 1951 there were 679 reported abortions. In 2014 there were 926,240 reported abortions in the United States. In 1951 one way of having an unreported abortion was a self-induced chemical abortion. A self-induced abortion (or self-induced miscarriage) is an abortion performed by the pregnant woman herself. Ingesting abortifacients, vitamin C mega dosage, pennyroyal or other substances would induce a miscarriage.

This baby did not bring the joy it should have. Out of desperation and pressure, mom did take a self-inducing abortion drug. Miraculously the drug that should have induced a miscarriage didn't! But what it did do was make my mom extremely sick. She pleaded with Dad not to make her do this again and he agreed.

In July 1951 my dad divorced his first wife and eighteen days later in August, my mom and dad were married.

On December 1, 1951, their baby boy was born. They named him Todd Gregory Greiner. The miracle hand of God was upon me in my mother's womb! The words of Jeremiah the prophet proved to be true in this young baby's life also!...

"Before I formed you in the womb, I knew you, before you were born I set you apart" (Jer. 1:5 NIV).

Set Apart from My Mother's Womb

God wasn't through!

"For I know the plans I have for you," declares the LORD, "plans to prosper you and not to harm you, plans to give you hope and a future" (Jer. 29:11 NIV).

It was 1958, and the Lord used this young six-year-old boy to have an impact on his mother. I had been sick and was lying on the living room couch. Mom was reading a story to me from a children's Bible storybook. A crowd had gathered to listen to Jesus. There was a young boy in the crowd that wanted to get close to Jesus but was having a hard time because of the large gathering.

Suddenly, I stood to my feet on the couch, walked to the arm of the sofa, looked at mom and began to preach to her at six years old! I said, "Mom, the little boy did not have to fight through the crowd to see Jesus because he saw Jesus in his heart and that's where Jesus lives!" Mom couldn't believe it! Not only had I been sick and not able to get off the couch, but here I was standing and talking about Jesus without having any prior understanding of who Jesus was! Remarkably, with tears flowing down her face, my mom watched and listened as I kept talking about Jesus!

Jesus used this experience to begin opening the heart of my mom. She started to visit a small Methodist Church in town. It was November 12, 1958, on a Wednesday night, that the Lord Jesus Christ made Himself real to her in a life-changing way. The layman was to speak on prayer, but he spoke about Jesus Christ and our desperate need for Him. When he spoke of Pontius Pilate asking the crowd what he should do with Jesus because he could find no fault in him, the crowd cried in one accord, "Crucify him! Crucify him!" She saw herself standing there with the crowd and in her heart screaming "Crucify him." She knew then that her heart was desperately wicked. She left that night with her heart broken by the Holy Spirit.

The next day, November 13, she asked Jesus Christ to forgive her of her sins and asked Him into her heart. That was the beginning of her new life!

Do I remember this experience? No, not at all. Growing up, my mom related this story many times; I will never forget it. I'm sharing this story of her salvation sixty years after it happened. My mom and dad have both gone on to be with the Lord.

Adultery has consequences. However, if we ask God for forgiveness, He is gracious to forgive and heal fractured relationships.

Dad's divorce had devastating results on his family. Going through a divorce is difficult for children at any age. His son, Larry, was fourteen years old when the divorce happened, and it destroyed their relationship. It wasn't until after Larry's firstborn son was born ten years later that Larry and our dad were reunited.

Growing up, I didn't even know I had a brother until my dad was reunited with Larry. Reconciliation is a gift from God. After all these years my sister Carol, my brother Larry and I genuinely love and respect each other.

I was an illegitimate child and consider the stigma that can bring. God in His great mercy laid His hand upon my life, and even though my mother out of desperation tried a self-induced chemical abortion, God had other plans!

2

Choices have Consequences

How old do we need to be before choices, whether good or bad, have an impact on our lives?

I vividly remember when I was twelve years old and the Lord first spoke to my heart. This is what He said… "Will you give me your life?"

Throughout this book I will share experiences when the Lord clearly spoke to me about something. This should not be surprising. Throughout my life I have met people who had a persona of being "super spiritual." It has always been my prayer and deliberate purpose to not be a person who comes across that way. But it would be an injustice to the Living God to deny or demean hearing the voice of God.

I almost dedicated a chapter explaining what it means to hear the voice of God. I decided that it was not necessary to do that, but this is a good place for me to mention hearing His voice because I will refer to hearing Him often throughout this book. It does not mean to literally hear an audible voice, even though God could do that if He chose to. I have never heard the audible voice of God, but I've heard Him speak in my inner spirit when it was His sovereign will to do so. I have never heard God speak to me on my terms (when I wanted), it has always been on His terms… His timing and in His own way.

AN AMAZING JOURNEY

The real question is not about God speaking, but about us listening…

In the gospel of John, Jesus is speaking about His sheep (His people) hearing His voice…

"…the sheep listen to his voice. He calls his own sheep by name and leads them out. When he has brought out all his own, he goes on ahead of them, and his sheep follow him because they know his voice" (Jo. 10:3,4 NIV).

Eight times in the book of Revelation we hear these words…

"He who has an ear, let him hear what the Spirit says to the churches"

(Rev. 2:7 NIV).

Hearing the voice of the Lord should come first and foremost through His Word, but He also speaks to our inner man (spirit) if we will listen. Let me reiterate, hearing His voice in our inner spirit comes by His sovereign choosing and not ours! Much could be shared about this but that's not the intention of the book. I believe that the experiences I share will be self-evident that God still speaks to His people!

Now, back to when I was twelve years old—when the Lord first spoke to my heart and asked… "Will you give me your life?" What was my response?

Nothing!

Even though I absolutely knew this was the Lord speaking to me at my young age I did not respond at all. No response was a loud response!

After we read about the birth of Jesus Christ in the Gospels, we do not see Him again until He is twelve years old. A twelve-year-old person can be very sensitive to the things of God.

"Every year his parents went to Jerusalem for the Feast of the Passover. When he was twelve years old, they went up to the Feast, according to the custom. After the Feast was over, while

Choices have Consequences

his parents were returning home, the boy Jesus stayed behind in Jerusalem, but they were unaware of it. Thinking he was in their company, they traveled on for a day. Then they began looking for him among their relatives and friends. When they did not find him, they went back to Jerusalem to look for him. After three days they found him in the temple courts, sitting among the teachers, listening to them and asking them questions. Everyone who heard him was amazed at his understanding and his answers. When his parents saw him, they were astonished. His mother said to him, "Son, why have you treated us like this? Your father and I have been anxiously searching for you." "Why were you searching for me?" he asked. "Didn't you know I had to be in my Father's house?" 50But they did not understand what he was saying to them" (Lk. 2:41-50 NIV).

When I was twelve years old, I knew without a doubt that the Holy Spirit had spoken to my heart, yet I refused to say "Yes" when the Lord asked me if I would give Him my life.

My mother gave her life to Jesus Christ in November 1958. For five years my mom was earnestly praying that her son would grow up to be a man of God. Even though I was so young she understood the importance of prayer and God's hand being on my life from a young age. The Lord answered her prayer and He spoke to my heart, but I turned away from His gentle invitation for me to give Him my life.

I started the chapter with this question… "How old do we need to be before choices, whether good or bad, have an impact on our lives?" The Bible does not give a specific age to answer this question, but the Bible does say this…

"Anyone, then, who knows the good he ought to do and doesn't do it, sins" (Ja. 4:17 NIV).

The Bible also says this…

"For the wages of sin is death, but the gift of God is eternal life in Christ Jesus our Lord" (Rom. 6:23 NIV).

Did I know the "good to do" when the Lord spoke to me about giving Him my life; I did! But I did not do it! Is that the first time I sinned as a twelve-year-old boy? Of course not. I understood right and wrong, good, and bad, and at this young age I had already started making many wrong choices.

Choices Do Have Consequences. For the next nine years of my life, I had an emptiness that I didn't understand until I became twenty-one. If I had said yes to the Holy Spirit when He asked me to give Him my life, I can only imagine what those early years of my life would have been like, but by saying nothing, I said no.

What's important to understand is that for the next nine years I never stopped believing in God. Was I a Christian? I thought I was. But I was not.

Right before I became a Christian, I became a professing atheist. God used that atheistic thinking in my life because no one can really be saved until they know for sure they are lost. During these nine years I did not live as a Christian, yet I thought I was. Truthfully, this is typical of most of the population in the world. Most people believe in a God but are not saved and not going to heaven…

*"Enter through the **narrow gate**. For **wide is the gate and broad is the road** that leads to destruction, and **many** enter through it. But small is the gate and narrow the road that leads to life, and only a few find it" (Mat. 7:13,14 NIV).*

Those are not my words; this is what the Bible says! This is completely contrary to our worldly thinking. We think it's just the opposite, that there are only a few that will go to hell, but the majority will go to heaven. That's not what the Bible says. The road leading to destruction is broad and MANY take

Choices have Consequences

that road. The road that leads to eternal life is NARROW and only a few choose to take that road. I was guilty of being that person who believed in a God, but I was going straight down the broad road that leads to destruction.

3

Years of Wandering

"A person with good sense is respected; a treacherous person is headed for destruction. Wise people think before they act; fools don't— and even brag about their foolishness" (Pro. 13:15-17 NLT).

Choices Do Have Consequences. For the next nine years of my life, I had an emptiness that I didn't understand until I became twenty-one. If I had said yes to the Holy Spirit when He asked me to give Him my life, I can only imagine what those early years of my life would have been like, but by saying nothing, I said no.

I was one month shy of being seven years old when my mom gave her life to Jesus Christ. I did not grow up with a single parent but did grow up with two parents who looked at life in complete contrast from each other. My mother was not a "religious" person; she was a genuine Christian who loved the Lord Jesus Christ with all her heart. My dad on the other hand, wanted to have nothing to do with God or a godly life. What young boy wants to grow up being like his mom?

I would not have used these words as a child, but in my young childhood I viewed Christianity as being feminine. I loved my mom, but her Christianity embarrassed me. I am now so ashamed to even say those words, but I want to be completely honest with my testimony. My dad and I had a troubled relationship but nonetheless he was my dad and he was a man, and that's what I wanted to be. Since he didn't follow God why should I?

My grandfather was hard on my dad and my dad was hard on me. In a previous chapter I shared when my mom became pregnant with me and she attempted a self-induced abortion by being pressured to do so from my dad.

Even though I did not have a "heart-to-heart" relationship with my dad I greatly admired and respected him. He was a very talented man. When I was a young boy, he had his own carpenter shop; he specialized in building cabinets. His talent went far beyond just building cabinets. He could build anything. I remember three different boats he built.

I'm giving my dad a helping hand as he's building this inboard motorboat

AN AMAZING JOURNEY

This is what the finished project looked like

When I was still a baby, my dad bought an old brick barn for the four of us to live in (dad, mom, my sister (half-sister), and myself). The barn was built around the same time the Charles Tiedemann mill was built between 1860-1861. Mr. Tiedemann owned both properties; there were railroad tracks that went from the barn up to the mill. The barn and the mill were two of the oldest properties in O'Fallon.

Charles Tiedemann mill

Years of Wandering

Tiedemann mill has catastrophic fire in November 1972

AN AMAZING JOURNEY

When you walked inside the barn you stepped onto a dirt floor. The second floor did not have a ceiling which made it possible to add another floor, which dad did. Now it became a three-story barn. We had to have a place to live so dad took part of the third story and made an apartment. The first and second floors were entirely used for his workshop.

The original barn before dad started converting it into our house

The barn became a beautiful house

Years of Wandering

This is a funny story about the barn. I was in second grade and time had come for a parent-teacher conference at the school. As the teacher was explaining my progress, or lack thereof, she also mentioned this… "Mrs. Greiner, I'm concerned about Todd's imagination, it's very vivid and he has a way of convincing the other children about some far-fetched ideas. For instance, the other day he told the kids that he lived in a barn. He was proud of it and convincing." Hiding her laughter, my mom replied, "He does live in a barn."

Grade school was very difficult for me. I went through the second grade twice. Concentration was challenging and I was convinced from childhood that I was not cut out for school. I was constantly getting in trouble.

ADHD was first mentioned in 1902. British pediatrician Sir George Still described it as "an abnormal defect of moral control in children. " He found that some affected children could not control their behavior the way a typical child would, but they were still intelligent. ADHD may have been first mentioned in 1902, but in 1958 in O'Fallon, Illinois they'd never heard of it! My ADHD (unknown to her and my doctor) was driving my mom crazy.

She took me to the doctor seeking help. She explained my nonstop energy, and lack of concentration for any schoolwork. The doctor gave her a prescription and said, "Try this." A couple of weeks went by with no change, so she made another appointment. When she came back to the physician she said, "Doctor, I have been consistently giving Todd the medicine and it has not helped at all.

Mrs. Greiner!" he declared, "that medicine was meant for you!"

Below, I have inserted two report cards. One is from the first time I tried getting through second grade, then I include the report card from the second time I attempted second grade. What an improvement!

On the first report card is where I had the most consistent marks: Wastes Time; Work Carelessly Done; Gives up Too Easily; Inattentive; Work Is Irregular; Capable of Doing Better. These are not areas in which you want high marks!

It's obvious that my parents and my teacher thought it best to hold me back and try second grade again. My next try at second grade resulted in the best report card I had during my entire time in school. Most kids are enticed by their parents to get good grades by offering their child either some special privilege or special payment for getting an "A." I'm the only one I know in school who was promised a monetary incentive if I would get just a "C." My parents still saved a lot of money!

Report card from first attempt at second grade (1958, 1959)

Years of Wandering

Report card from second attempt at second grade (1959, 1960)

Poor performance in school never improved. Some of the worst days I can remember were the days I had to bring home my report card. Looking back, I'm not sure what my mother dreaded the most, seeing another bad report card or knowing the reaction my dad would have. After I became a Christian I really loved my dad, but when I was young I was afraid of him. Knowing what some children face with an abusive parent was not the situation with me. Yes, his discipline was harsh, and he never knew how to show me love, but he didn't physically abuse me. Nonetheless, I would rather hide in a cave than show my dad my report card! Report cards came out every nine weeks. He honestly thought if he grounded me to my bedroom every night for nine weeks that I would improve, so that's what he did. The only problem was it didn't work. Concentration was so difficult for me. And I had convinced myself that I would never do well in school. So, being grounded to my bedroom every night I never studied because I didn't know how to do it.

Things only grew worse when I reached high school. My relationship with my dad grew worse until finally it exploded one evening during dinner. Dinner was never a happy time for us. More times than not, my dad would come home from work frustrated and angry. It had been years since my dad had his cabinet shop even though he still did cabinet work on the side but for years now he'd been one of the superintendents of a large construction company. Their type of work was building hospitals, schools, and large business facilities. I know he had an enormous amount of responsibility and stress, but the stress reliever was letting it out on his family. On this particular evening the situation was ripe for an explosion. He was in a bad mood and so was I.

Most families look back at dinner gatherings as a pleasant memory, not so with my family. It seemed like my mom could never get the dinner right, even though she was an excellent cook. Something was either too hot or too cold, not spiced like he wanted it, etc.

This was one of those unpleasant dinner gatherings. Dad began by finding fault with something about my mom and then he started lecturing me. I was eighteen years old at the time. He started lecturing me about my girlfriend and our relationship. I exploded! What happened next broke my mother's heart. I jumped up from the table pointed my finger in my dad's face and said, "I've taken all that I'm going to take from you!" He jumped up and we both started swinging fists. I won't go into the ugly details, but it was heart crushing for my mother, and terrible for my dad and me. He threatened to throw me out of the house, and I said, "Save your breath, I'm leaving on my own." I had my own car at the time, but he warned me sternly to leave without my car. I did.

I walked to a friend's house and asked him to take me to my girlfriend's house. He dropped me off at her home and I went inside and shared the situation with her and her family. They felt terrible about what happened but made it crystal clear that staying at their home was not an option. I asked my girlfriend to drive me to my brother's house.

I wrote in a previous chapter about the relationship between my brother and our dad. After my dad's divorce from my brother's mother, ten years went by with no relationship between the two of them at all. When I shared the situation about dad and me with my brother Larry, he also felt terrible about it and shared his heart with me. He stated that the relationship was improving between him and Dad, and if he took me into his home it would only aggravate the relationship between him and Dad. I understood.

I asked my girlfriend to take me to my sister and brother-in-law's house. The three of us were close. I loved them very much. I explained the situation to them and their reaction amazed me. My brother-in-law, David, said "Todd, I consider you a brother, I understand how your dad can be and you are welcome to live with us." Wow, they both took such a risk in doing that. They knew by opening their home to me would jeopardize their relationship with Dad, but did it anyway.

This took place during my senior year in high school. They both agreed to allow me to use my sister's car until we could figure out how to get my car back. If my dad had purchased my car and told me I couldn't take it, it would have made sense, but the fact was I bought it myself. My dad finally agreed and allowed me to take my car.

AN AMAZING JOURNEY

On the first of December, my senior year, I got a job working at Roesch Enamel & Manufacturing Company located in Belleville, Illinois. This was not a part-time job; I worked a full 40 hours per week in addition to going to high school. My last class in school was over at 2:00 p.m. and I had to be at work by 3:00. I went to school in O'Fallon and went to work in Belleville; I had to move fast to be at work on time. I studied in high school like I did in grade school, which was very little. I would rather work forty hours at Roesch Enamel than study anyway. I got off work at 11:00 p.m.

I was in high school when I began to smoke and drink. It was an absolute miracle by the grace of God that alcohol did not take my life during my high school years. Before I gave my life to the Lord I was in three car accidents, all of them alcohol-related. One happened while I was still in high school, and the other two happened after I joined the military.

After being away from home for a few months my dad and I finally made amends. I use that word because neither one of us genuinely asked for forgiveness. I know we both regretted what happened, but both of us were too proud to offer a genuine apology. Things were improving and we got along better. Then, I did such a stupid thing...

On one particular night of drinking, I ended up in the city jail. I did not drink because I enjoyed the taste of alcohol; I hated the taste and drank for one reason only, to get drunk. After getting drunk, I acted like an idiot. On this night after spending the entire evening drinking as much as I could I became very belligerent. Belligerent enough for someone to call the police. The police officer who arrested me knew who I was and knew my dad. After taking me to jail he told me the only way I was going to get out was for me to call my dad and for him to come and bail me out. I was not about to do that! I had just returned home and my dad and I were walking together on thin ice; if I called him from jail, it's hard telling what would happen. Finally, after spending hours in jail I gave in and called my dad. I couldn't believe it, he came and got me out of jail and didn't have much to say. Before we left a date was set for me to appear before a judge.

The county courthouse was in a neighboring town. I will never forget this day when my dad and I went together for me to appear before the judge. It was getting late in the day, and I was one of the last to appear before the judge. I was fined a certain amount of money that had to be paid right then or I would go to jail. I'm not sure what my dad and I were thinking, the truth is, neither one of us were thinking clearly. The fine had to be paid by cash, and neither one of us had enough cash with us. It's strange how the Lord can take something so bad and use it for something good. Since this was on a Friday afternoon, if the court did not receive the payment of the fine within approximately forty-five minutes, I would have to spend the weekend in jail.

To leave from the courthouse, drive home and back to the courthouse would take every bit of an hour at best. How my dad did it I'll never know, but he made it back in time to pay the fine and keep me out of jail. I was so grateful! All my dad said to me was that I would have to pay him back the money.

I had a good relationship with my mom but did not embrace the relationship she had with God. I had a very twisted concept of what it meant to be a Christian. I would never volunteer that I was a Christian, but if asked I would say I was. It was typical of the largest percentage of people in America today. I believed in the existence of God, so I convinced myself this made me a Christian.

"The fool says in his heart, "There is no God" (Ps. 14:1 NIV).

I was even a bigger fool than the fool mentioned in the verse above. What's worse: saying that there is no God or saying that there is a God, but in reality, you have no room for Him in your heart? This is the most damning ideology in the world today. There are very few true atheists throughout the entire world. Most of the world believes in a God. The verse below had my name written all over it...

"They claim to know God, but by their actions they deny him. They are detestable, disobedient and unfit for doing anything good" (Titus 1:16 NIV).

Yes, I believed in Jesus and believed the Bible because my mother had convinced me that much was true. I often tell people how heaven can be missed by fourteen inches. That's the average distance from the brain to the heart. Believing that Jesus came to this earth, went to the cross, and died for our sins will never get you into heaven. That's nothing more than just head knowledge and it fit me perfectly.

"The word is near you; it is in your mouth and in your heart," that is, the word of faith we are proclaiming: That if you confess with your mouth, "Jesus is Lord," and believe in your heart that God raised him from the dead, you will be saved" (Rom. 10:8-10 NIV).

The above verse from the book of Romans makes it crystal clear. *"...if you confess with your mouth, "Jesus is Lord..."* I could never say that, and never wanted to! As a matter of fact, read this...

"Therefore, I tell you that no one who is speaking by the Spirit of God says, "Jesus be cursed," and no one can say, "Jesus is Lord," except by the Holy Spirit" (1 Cor. 12:3 NIV).

I have witnessed this many times, persons will not say "Jesus Is Lord over all" unless they sincerely mean it. I couldn't say it, nor did I want to. It's very easy to say the word "God" and also to say that you believe in God, but a person will not and cannot say sincerely "Jesus is Lord" unless it comes from the Holy Spirit living within a person!

Back to Romans chapter 10 "...*and believe in your heart...*" This is where the fourteen inches comes in; the Scripture makes it clear that "believing" resulting in salvation must come from the heart. All I had was a concept of believing, twisted as it was, that came from my head, not my heart.

Unfortunately, I still had a few more years to go before I'd give my life to Jesus Christ and become a genuine Christian.

4

Atheism Was Part of God's Plan

"Only fools say in their hearts, 'There is no God.' They are corrupt, and their actions are evil; not one of them does good!" (Ps. 14:1 NLT)

I was a fool and like most fools, did not see it and would not admit it.

What does an atheist and a religious person (who doesn't really know God) have in common? … Neither one will spend eternity in heaven—both are lost!

God knows how to get our attention. He will use whatever measures He desires. This is how he got my attention.

Mothers who walk with Jesus Christ have mountain-moving faith. My mom certainly did. After she gave her life to the Lord, she labored in prayer daily for her family. From my early age, my mom sensed that God had a calling upon my life.

"The earnest prayer of a righteous person has great power and produces wonderful results." (Ja. 5:16 NLT).

I know there were countless times that her faith was greatly tested, especially when she watched my life descend deeper and deeper into sin. She stood firm in the face of great adversity.

"So, let's not get tired of doing what is good. At just the right

time we will reap a harvest of blessing if we don't give up" (Gal. 6:9 NLT).

She never gave up!

I graduated from high school in 1970. I barely made it through twelve years of school and the idea of going to college wasn't even in the picture. I wanted to leave O'Fallon, Illinois.

My brother owned a small engine repair shop where he sold lawnmowers and small lawn tractors. I enjoyed working for him. When I was fifteen years old, I could completely overhaul a small engine. A man and his wife lived next door to the shop, and he was a chief petty officer in the United States Coast Guard, stationed in St. Louis. He would often come over to the shop to get a drink out of the soda machine. It seemed like he took a special interest in me and told me a lot about the Coast Guard. He was not a recruiter, but he was doing a good job at being one. I was convinced that joining the United States Coast Guard was something I wanted to do. This all took place prior to my graduation from high school.

After I graduated from high school, "I" had it all figured out. I talked with a USCG recruiter in St. Louis, and he told me about enlisting under the "buddy system." This meant, two young men would sign up together and were guaranteed to stay together through boot camp. However, after boot camp there would not be any guarantee that we'd get the same duty station. Our enlistment date was set for July 20, 1970. I was fired up and ready to go, but my friend who was to enlist with me got cold feet and changed his mind at the last minute. I was not deterred, so on July 20, I boarded a plane to Alameda, California.

After boot camp in Alameda I was sent to New York to be stationed on Governors Island. Governors Island is a 172-acre

AN AMAZING JOURNEY

island in New York Harbor, within the New York City municipality of Manhattan. I was sent to school to be a radarman. Governors Island is what the Statue of Liberty is looking at.

After radar school I received orders to go to Baltimore, Maryland to be stationed on the United States Coast Guard Cutter Southwind 280. The ship was an icebreaker, and I spent the next twenty-seven months going to places that very few people have ever gone. I made two cruises above the Arctic Circle and one cruise into Antarctica.

The USCGC Southwind had an amazing history.

The icebreaker was transferred to the Soviet Union under the terms of lend-lease on 25 March 1945 at Tacoma, Washington. On that date, the Southwind's commanding officer, CAPT Richard M. Hoyle, USCG, turned over control of the vessel over to CDR A. M. Khokhlov, USSRN, who was the designated Soviet representative. He was renamed Admiral Makarov (a famous Russian mariner and naval architect recognized as father of the modern icebreaker) by the Soviets. The ship operated in the Russian merchant marine for four-and-one-half years before the Soviet Union returned her to the United States at Yokosuka, Japan, on 28 December 1949.

My duty on the Southwind began on March 5, 1971. The Arctic cruise just prior to my arrival for duty left a historical mark in icebreaker history. On August 15, 1970, she reached 83° 01' North, the northernmost penetration into the Arctic Basin by a U.S. icebreaker to date. On that same cruise the Southwind visited a seaport in Murmansk, Russia. The Soviets returned an Apollo training capsule (BP-1227) that they had recovered at sea. Apparently, the U.S. Air Force Aerospace Rescue and Recovery personnel who were using the 9,500-pound capsule for training lost it at sea near the Azores in February 1969. It was recovered by a Soviet fishing trawler. The Southwind, after first sustaining a "bump" by a Soviet icebreaker while departing Murmansk for home, carried the capsule back to the U.S. and deposited it at Norfolk before ending her cruise at Baltimore on 17 November 1970.

Southwind, 1944 (WAGB 280; ex-Atka; Admiral Makarov)

During my twenty-seven months of sea duty as a radarman on the USCGC Southwind and USCGC Edisto I had the privilege to visit these cities and countries:

Oslo, Norway.

Bergen, Norway. Bergen is considered one of the most northern cities of the world.

Reykjavík, Iceland. Reykjavik is Iceland's capital and houses over two-thirds of the population.

Keflavík, Iceland.

AN AMAZING JOURNEY

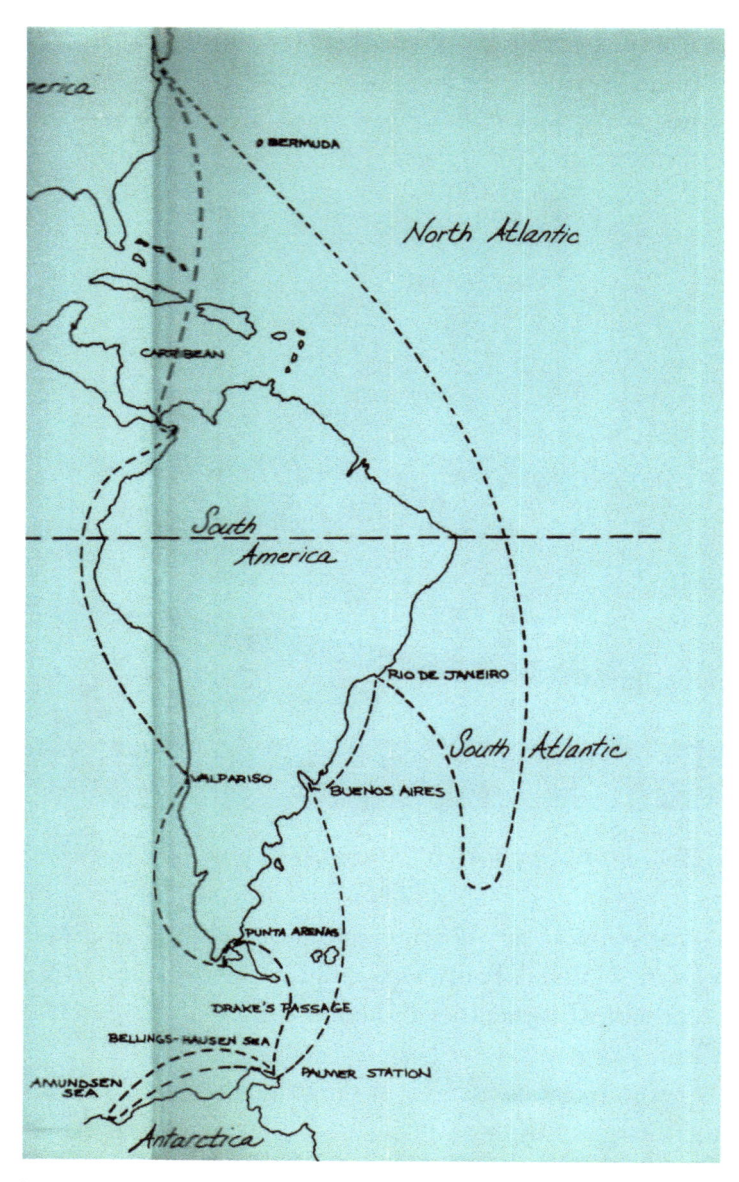

This is the route we took from Baltimore, Maryland into Antarctica and back home again. December 1, 1971 – April 2, 1972.

Atheism Was Part of God's Plan

Thule, Greenland. Thule Air Base is the United States Air Force's northernmost base - (76 32' North latitude, 68 50' West longitude) located 695 miles north of the Arctic Circle, and 947 miles south of the North Pole on the northwest side of the island of Greenland.

Panama Canal which took approximately nine hours to pass through.

Panama City, Panama

Lima, Peru.

Valparaiso, Chile.

Punta Arenas, Chile. Punta Arenas is the southernmost city of the world.

Buenos Aires, Argentina.

Rio de Janeiro, Brazil.

Our ship took extensive time doing scientific survey in Antarctica.

My sea duty on the Southwind was serving a greater purpose than I ever realized. God is so patient in strategically working His plan. I had been walking in spiritual blindness throughout my young life and I desperately needed an eye-opening experience yet was oblivious to it. You can't be saved until you know you are lost. This is what God was patiently making real to me.

I will never forget an episode that took place in New York City while I was still in radar school. I was sitting at a bar drinking with some friends. How the subject came up, I'll never know, but someone brought up the subject of God. The question was asked "do any of you believe in God?" I will never forget my answer… "You're blankety-blank right #!@*&% I believe in God!" Not only is the person who says there is no God a fool, the way I responded back to the question showed that I was an even greater fool!

I grew up never doubting that God existed. My mom had taught me about Jesus and what He did on the cross. In "my own way" I understood that Jesus died for our sins without requiring a response from me. I thought if I believed that Jesus existed, then that made me a Christian. I viewed my mom as being fanatical. I thought of myself as a Christian, yet my life gave evidence of just the opposite.

Satan had me in his grip. If it wasn't for the fact that I had a mother at home fervently praying and fighting a spiritual battle for my soul, Satan would have succeeded with his purpose on this earth…

"The thief comes only to steal and kill and destroy…" (Jo. 10:10 NIV)

God had to show me how lost I really was since I had such a distorted idea of Christianity. God had a great plan to expose that distortion.

Atheism.

Tight quarters is an understatement. The size of the Southwind was 269 feet long and 83 feet wide. The crew was close to 250 men. When we left on deployment, we would not return for about 4 ½ months. It's amazing that the crew does not try to kill each other, being confined for that length of time in such a small space. On the contrary, you develop close friendships. You are not a group of men going off to war, but you are a group of men working together for the mission.

It's been over 50 years since I arrived for duty on the Southwind. I still stay in contact with a good friend I served with on the ship. Another such friend God used in an unusual way to bring me to an eye-opening experience.

His name was Richard, he was nicknamed "Pic." Pic was a shortened version of his long Italian last name. We were good friends, and he also had my admiration because he was quite intelligent. Remember, I'm the one who barely made it through high school. This man had two college degrees. I'm the one who believed in God (though I was not saved). Pic was an atheist.

The way he looked at life fascinated me. I had never met anyone like him. Over months of being together on the ship he was discipling me without me realizing it. I didn't like reading, but he insisted that I read this book… "The Naked Ape." This is a description of the book…

"We were all gearing up for the summer of love when, in 1967, Desmond Morris's The Naked Ape took us by storm. Its pitch was that humans really were just apes, and much of our behavior could be understood in terms of animal behavior and its evolution."

Pic succeeded! I denounced my distorted belief and accepted atheism as truth. Now I was really being discipled. God had me right where I needed to be! When I renounced my so-called "faith" that was a great step forward. Embracing atheism was better than where I was. I thought I had been a Christian and yet I was the furthest thing from being one.

"These are the words of the Amen, the faithful and true witness, the ruler of God's creation. I know your deeds, that you are neither cold nor hot. I wish you were either one or the other! So, because you are lukewarm—neither hot nor cold—I am about to spit you out of my mouth" (Rev. 3:14-16 NIV).

Wow, I had been nothing but spit!

As time went on, I became more convinced that religion was a crutch and atheism was scientific. I had convinced myself that I would share all my newfound insight with my mom. I was so deceived; I had planned to get with my mom and explain to her where she was wrong and hopefully, she would also denounce her faith and her eyes would be opened like mine.

The right time had come. I acquired two weeks of leave and decided to use this time to visit my family. I hadn't been home long and could hardly wait to be alone with my mom and share with her my brilliant insight.

The time was perfect; "Mom, we need to talk."

"Okay Todd, I'm ready when you are," she replied, not knowing what it was about.

I will never forget the scene—it's like a video being played in my mind. My mom and I were in the living room sitting across from each other. "Mom, I have something I need to share with you that is very important, and I know that it will upset you, but I'm asking that you would please be open-minded."

"Okay hon," she replied.

So, I proceeded with my speech.

My mom was very discerning and wise. She knew that she was facing off with the devil himself. I'm not saying I was the devil, but I was a tool in his hands! It was astonishing how she kept her cool.

I didn't know this until after the fact, but the whole time I was talking she was fervently praying in her spirit without her lips moving. How she kept a smile on her face I don't know, but she did. I was completely unaware of her fervent praying, but it was doing a powerful work. The more I tried to explain myself the more confused I became. I was thinking to myself, "I wish Pic was here, I really need him!" I felt like someone had taken a vacuum cleaner and held it right up against my ear. It was sucking all my thoughts straight into the vacuum! With my face full of frustration, I looked at my mom and said, "Just forget it! I can't explain to you how I feel or what I'm trying to say!"

Atheism Was Part of God's Plan

With a grin on my mom's face, she said, "I'm listening honey, do your best, keep talking." This meeting that I had planned for such a long time ended in my own personal turmoil—exactly where God wanted me to be.

That evening I had a date with a girl I had been corresponding with via mail for months. I used her for a sounding board venting my frustration. Finally, sometime after midnight she said, "Todd, I'm sorry, you're confused, but I don't know what to say or how to help."

The next morning my life was changed forever.

This will be etched in my memory until the day that I depart this earth! I'm not sure when I woke up, I slept in longer than normal. I was sitting on the edge of my bed and had an overwhelming sense of emptiness.

The same voice that spoke to me when I was twelve years old spoke again. It was not audible, I wasn't struck with lightning, there was no writing on the wall, but I heard His voice speak to my heart as if it were audible… ***"I am real and what are you going to do about it?"***

I knew immediately who spoke these words to my heart. I did not question these words for a moment. I got up, put my clothes on and walked into the kitchen where my mom was doing dishes. I tapped my mom on the shoulder and said, "Mom, we've got to talk!" Just yesterday we had a talk which ended in my own personal frustration and turmoil. This was different.

As she turned and looked at me, I said, "Mom, I'm dead!"

"What do you mean?" she replied.

I stretched my arms out straight to each side like a cross. Again, I said, "Mom, I'm dead!" I reached over with my right hand and pinched my left arm. "Mom, I can feel this, my body hasn't died, but I'm dead inside."

Tears began to flow down her cheeks.

AN AMAZING JOURNEY

"Mom, for the first time in my life I understand something. I'm the biggest fool that ever lived! God is real, and I have completely rejected Him. This foolish talk about atheism is utterly stupid. I have never understood what I understand now. I need God so bad. I want God in my life, and I don't know what to do."

My mom could have shared with me what we call "The Roman Road." She could've sat me down and preached to me for an hour. She could've told me how ridiculous I've been for so many years. But she didn't do any of that. With tears still streaming down her face and with overwhelming love she looked straight into my eyes and said "Sweetheart, go back into your bedroom and tell Jesus how you feel. Tell Him what you just told me. He died on the cross for all your sins and loves you. Confess your sins to Him and ask Jesus into your heart."

That's all she said. I'm not sure if it took even a minute.

I did exactly what she told me to do. I shut the door and dropped across the bed and began to pour my heart out to God.

"Jesus, my heart and my soul are completely black with sin. I'm not worthy to even talk to you. Please forgive me and cleanse me. I don't know how you could even want me, but I give myself to you from my head to my toes."

I will never forget the image that came to my mind. I felt like for years I had been lowering a bucket into an open well waiting for the bucket to reach some fresh water that would revive me and give me meaning and purpose. When I finished pouring my heart out to God it was like I heard this gentle splash as the bucket finally reached the water.

My mom shared this story with so many people, these were her words… "I saw my son walk into his bedroom looking like a corpse. After time had elapsed, I then saw my new son walk out of his bedroom looking like a completely different person. He glowed."

This radical life-changing experience happened in February of 1973.

5

A New Guy on the Ship

"That if you confess with your mouth, "Jesus is Lord," and believe in your heart that God raised him from the dead, you will be saved" (Rom. 10:9 NIV).

I had never read the Bible; I only had heard a few things from my mother. But the One who authored the Bible was now living in my heart. It wouldn't be long before I would start consuming the Word of God. Without my knowledge of the above verse, the Holy Spirit was about to make this very real within me, removing shame and embarrassment.

Let me explain.

After my life-changing conversion it was time for me to go back to my ship. My mother and brother-in-law took me to the airport. I checked in my luggage and took a bag on board with me. Without my knowledge my mom put a few things in my bag. One was a book entitled, "We Would See Jesus." In the past my mom would send me packages. She'd include snacks and other items I liked but she seemed to always include literature or a book about the Lord. If it had a cover that looked too "Christian" I would quickly place it somewhere no one could see it. Even though I "believed in God" (before my atheistic journey) I was fulfilling this Scripture…

A New Guy on the Ship

"If anyone is ashamed of me and my words, the Son of Man will be ashamed of him when he comes in his glory..." (Lk.9:26 NIV).

That was me!

I boarded the plane.

I was one of the first ones on the plane, so I had a good choice of seats. I was flying second class, but I was able to be seated towards the front of that section. I selected my seat next to the window and had an open seat next to me towards the aisle. As soon as I sat down, I opened the bag to see what was in it. Lo and behold, there was the book, "We Would See Jesus!" Exactly the kind of book I would quickly hide if I had been on the ship. Shame and embarrassment were what I usually felt.

The cover of this book boldly portrayed a man on his knees, his hands clasped together in prayer looking up to heaven. Wow, I took the book out, looked at the cover and without any shame placed the book on the seat next to me and turned it in such a way that every person walking down the aisle could easily see the book! People walking down the aisle saw the seat, noticed the book, and then looked at me. I was grinning ear to ear. I said nothing out loud, but my body language was speaking loudly. This is what I was saying... "Yes, this book belongs to me, and this book is about Jesus. This man is humbling himself, praying, and seeking after God and so am I."

I never read Romans 10:9. I didn't even know there was such a verse. But I was confessing Jesus Christ as my Lord to every person walking down the aisle who would look at me!

I had not been back on the ship too long before my shipmates were thinking... "Who is this man? He says that his name is Todd Greiner, but this is not the Todd Greiner that I knew."

There was an obvious change. I had already spent twenty-three months on the ship. These men knew me by my filthy mouth and obsession with drinking. But I had changed.

My drinking buddies no longer hung out with me. My drinking stopped immediately, and later I would quit smoking. My filthy mouth also stopped immediately, so much so, it was as if I had a hard time communicating. When someone speaks with a filthy mouth, they have no idea how bad it sounds.

I've got to have a Bible!

There was another vivid picture in my mind: I've got to have a Bible! I remember the bookstore I went to looking for a Bible. I knew nothing about Bibles. The word "translation" was a foreign word to me. I didn't know the Bible came in various translations.

Here's what I so clearly remember…

I walked into the bookstore and asked the clerk where the section was that had a Bible. I had no idea how many Bibles there would be! Different sizes, colors, titles (translations), soft, hard. What was I going to do? The Lord knew exactly what I needed. As I was scanning the Bibles my eyes came across a green semi-hardbound Bible with the words "Living Bible."

Wow! That's the kind of Bible I want! I want a Bible that is alive and well!

Much later I learned that I had bought what is called a "paraphrased Bible." At the time I'm sure some well-meaning Christian friends would have done their best to talk me out of a paraphrased Bible. I'm so thankful I was by myself when I bought it! I could understand it and the Holy Spirit was using it in a great way.

I started devouring this Bible.

I would frequently call my mom just to talk. I told her what I bought, and she encouraged me and told me I needed

A New Guy on the Ship

to start reading in the New Testament. I had already started reading the Bible as a typical book; starting in the front of the book. But I took her advice and started with Matthew. I was loving it. I read Matthew, Mark, Luke and then part of John. I called my mom with this question... "Mom, is the entire Bible this same story written by different people?" I'm not kidding, I was serious. Not that I cared, I was enjoying the Gospels. "No," my mom said, "keep reading and you'll find out."

Being a radarman on the ship, I worked in a small room called Combat Information Center (CIC).

Radar screen in combat information Center (CIC). I spent many hours sitting in front of this radar screen plotting the course and speed of other ships and when the closest point of approach (CPA) would be to our ship. We would also use radar for spotting icebergs.

When the ship was not under deployment, CIC became my prayer closet and Bible study room. I was able to persuade three other men to join me in Bible study. It was such a joy to share what I was reading with a few of my friends. The Lord had not delivered me from cigarettes yet, and if someone came into CIC while we were having a Bible study, it looked like a charade. We would be having a Bible study in a smoke-filled room. I wanted to stop smoking so bad but what really struck me was that just a few weeks prior to this time my body and soul would have burned up in hell, and now only my lungs were burning up! God's grace and mercy was great! Within a few weeks I went from three packs of cigarettes a day to zero, and never went back.

6

Who Is the Holy Spirit?

"While Apollos was at Corinth, Paul took the road through the interior and arrived at Ephesus. There he found some disciples and asked them, "Did you receive the Holy Spirit when you believed?" They answered, "No, we have not even heard that there is a Holy Spirit"
(Acts 19:1-2 NIV).

Before you start this chapter, I want to share my heart about a few things. I'm not trying to prove anything. I'm not writing this book in the third person. These are all personal accounts being shared with absolute honesty. My first and foremost reason for writing this book is to glorify Jesus Christ. And this is not about personal achievements. I have no desire to argue personal theological viewpoints, but simply share what God has done in my life.

I identify in a small way with the man who was born blind, and Jesus miraculously healed him in a very unusual way, all recorded in John chapter 9.

When Jesus and his disciples came across this man the disciples asked Jesus this question…

"Rabbi, who sinned, this man or his parents, that he was born blind?" (Jo. 9:1 NIV)

Jesus answered...

"*Neither this man nor his parents sinned,*" said Jesus, "*but this happened so that the work of God might be displayed in his life*" (Jo. 9:3 NIV).

Wow, what a day this turned out to be!

Jesus spits on the ground, takes mud and puts it on the man's eyes. He told the man to go to the pool of Siloam and wash it off. The story doesn't say that the man even asked for healing. The man goes and washes in the pool and comes back with perfect eyesight!

He becomes the talk of the town. Some said he was the man who used to beg for help and others said he just looks like the man. But he kept saying, "I am the man!" Personal testimony is not always convincing.

You really should read this story, it is fantastic! The Pharisees argue with him, his parents want to distance themselves from him, and no one will take him at his word. The Pharisees argued that Jesus was a sinner for healing on the Sabbath. This is what the man replied...

"*Whether he is a sinner or not, I don't know. One thing I do know. I was blind but now I see!*" (Jo. 9:25 NIV)

The man who was healed did not want to argue theology but simply share what Jesus did. That's the same position I take.

My life-changing salvation happened in February 1973. On March 5, one month later, the Holy Spirit came upon me in a powerful way.

This is how it happened...

In the last chapter I shared about the small room I worked in located just below the bridge of the ship and called Combat Information Center (CIC). When the ship was underway this room was occupied 24/7 with one of us radarmen. But when

Who Is the Holy Spirit?

the ship was in port it was unnecessary to maintain a radar watch. It then became my prayer room.

For the last month the ship had not gone anywhere. I was able to spend literally hours in CIC praying and reading my Bible. I was earnestly crying out to God. No one was coaching me or discipling me, but the Holy Spirit was drawing me. The only way I understood what was happening is that I had an unquenchable thirst for God. I spent hours pouring out my heart and studying His Word. The only person I had to talk to was my mom during an occasional phone call.

Then it happened!

The morning of March 5, 1973 (this was exactly two years to the day that I boarded the ship) I was on watch between midnight and four in the morning. The day before I spent a lot of time in CIC. Sometime between midnight and four in the morning the Holy Spirit came upon me in a dynamic way. At the time when it happened, I had no idea what you would call this. Later I realized that I had experienced the infilling of the Holy Spirit. When someone is filled with the Holy Spirit it will be manifested in some form. People have tried to take this manifestation and put it in a box saying you must respond in a certain kind of way.

This is how the Holy Spirit manifested Himself to me…

I was filled with praise, but it came out in a different kind of praise. When we (petty officers) would stand watch, we would always have a lower rank shipmate standing watch with us. This person was called a "runner." He was with me when the Holy Spirit came upon me. He didn't notice anything, but I asked him for paper. I had to write down what the Holy Spirit was telling me! After writing this I sent it to my mom. She kept it for years and then it was returned to me. I still have it, and this is what I wrote verbatim…

AN AMAZING JOURNEY

March 5, 1973

"Oh, I am so happy tonight! My life has come back to me and like never before. This is not emotions, but the grace of our Lord. I have just one little part of what I will have if I stay with the Lord, and I know I will.

Mom, God has answered your prayers. This will give you joy as it has given me joy. Oh, I realize that Satan is angry tonight, and he will try his best to win me over, but mom, pray for me that I will be given strength.

These last few weeks can be compared to an earthworm. A ton of dirt had fallen on me and I kept climbing upward in darkness until I found the bright clear world. Up was the only way I could go. God has been very good to me tonight. I studied the Bible all day and He has shown me tonight what His grace will do if only I stay with Him. And oh, how I love Him! I can feel that He doesn't want me to become too overwhelmed and look for Him to give me other things. Patience, that is my homework. But He was so good to me, He is so good to me! Do you realize that I was only in real darkness for a couple of weeks when it could have been a couple of years? But the Lord knows that I am weak. Never again will I say that faith in yourself will make you strong. Without Him we aren't worthy of the dust that we were made of. My problem was that I was asking Him for the wrong things, He wants me to really get to know Him!

Why are we all so ignorant of His grace? What fools we are without Him. If my purpose in life is to make clay dolls out of mud that is what I will do and may the fruit of my faith be eaten by my brothers and sisters! Wow, life is great isn't it!

The world was so meaningless without Him. Satan can give you happiness too, but it can only be compared with one fraction of an inch to a million miles of the happiness you receive from our Lord and Savior.

Who Is the Holy Spirit?

I have so much to say but it will be said later. When you read this letter praise the Lord and pray to Him and thank Him because the words that are on this paper are from the Holy Spirit and not my own. When my mind is on evil thoughts I speak with my own ignorant tongue.

The Lord has a purpose for me, and I can't wait to be his servant. Only through your long nights of prayer has this happened. Thank you, my mother, I love you!

Tonight, I asked the Lord in a prayer for some more answers but only if it should be His will and it was just like a little child asking for a piece of candy and getting the candy store.

And oh, how I love my dad! If he ever knew that my love for him is so real. The Lord worked through him to give me my physical life. Dad never needs to give me anything material. He can only love the Lord and then he will love both of his sons the same. He will not favor one over the other. He will love them both the same and I know that this will happen, and it will happen soon. Praise the Lord now that it will happen and fall on your knees when it does and thank our father for what He has done. We will all join hands and cry for joy when it does because He answers prayer. Some say our family has had it bad and it has been painful for all, but the Lord saw our pain and will forgive our sins and give us abundant love and joy. How can we repay our Lord for what He has done and for what He will do?

Praise our Father and make Him happy. We are all His children. Oh, how I love Him! Oh Lord, forgive us when we do you wrong and our weak little minds are so small, yet you care for each one of us and your grace will never stop.

The Holy Spirit is working so fast that my hand can hardly keep up with Him!

Dad, you have worked so hard in your life, and you are tired, but the Lord will give you more strength than a twenty-year-old. I

AN AMAZING JOURNEY

pray to God that before I go, or you go to be with Him that we will have life together, and I know we will. But even if we shouldn't, our love can never be broken. We will work together and pray together, and we will play together. I love you so much dad, so very much.

I have been so rewarded, and you will be also. All the many years that we lived together and didn't even know each other would be rewarded. I wish I could kiss your cheek right now. So, dad, don't think that you are in a race to get things done. Drop your hammer and praise the Lord and when you go to pick it up again it will be gold plated and light as a feather. Oh dad, this is hard to do, but your first few words should be, Oh Lord, my father, I have sinned and the door to my heart has been closed but I now open the door and please come in. I'm not worthy to have you as Lord but you love the weakest, and you love the strongest so please take my soul and wash it. Take all that I have and give me your life and love.

Tell Him that you love your wife and your sons and your daughter, but you need His love to love as you should. Dad, this is real with me. Not here today and gone tomorrow. It's like riding a bicycle through sand, it is hard to peddle but don't give up. The kingdom of heaven is not easy to get into but once you are there your life begins.

Oh, how I praise the Lord that I'm so young, twenty-one and I have the rest of my life to be given in service to Him. This is all that God wants me to say for now, but I love you all."

This was amazing. I was twenty-one years old and less than one month as a born-again Christian. Each time I read this I can still feel the passion in which I was writing. The two sons referred to in the letter were my brother and I. Everything written prophetically in this letter came to pass. While I was in the service my dad prayed with a man to receive Christ as his

Who Is the Holy Spirit?

Savior. Today, my brother and his wife are strongly involved in a church in Florida. In the closing paragraph I mentioned that I have the rest of my life dedicated to serving Him. It has been over forty-nine years since this letter was written. I have never looked back! Serving Jesus is the priority of my life.

Another amazing event took place just a few days later.

Let me emphasize again that I have nothing to prove, and I am not trying to promote "pet doctrines" that some people believe. I am sharing this to authenticate what is often denied, criticized, and treated with contention.

I was a little over one month old in the Lord and had not started going to a church yet. What I'm about to share had nothing to do with any influence of any other individual on the face of this earth. I had not read this in the Bible yet and during the conversations with my mother this never came up. This was a sovereign work of the Holy Spirit that I wasn't even asking for. The only thing I was asking for repeatedly was, "Lord Jesus, I want more of you!" I had never hungered for anything in my twenty-one years on this earth like I was hungering for God Almighty.

"Ask and it will be given to you; seek and you will find; knock and the door will be opened to you. For everyone who asks receives; he who seeks finds; and to him who knocks, the door will be opened" (Mat. 7:7-8 NIV).

I was asking for more of Jesus and that is what He was about to do!

I was driving my car (I have no idea where I was going) and was worshiping the Lord with singing, praise and prayer and the most strange and wonderful thing happened that was completely unexplainable…!

"For if I pray in a tongue, my spirit prays, but my mind is

unfruitful. So what shall I do? I will pray with my spirit, but I will also pray with my mind; I will sing with my spirit, but I will also sing with my mind" (1 Cor. 14:14-15 NIV).

My language changed while I was singing! I have never been able to sing any song completely through because I never remember all the words. Whatever I was singing in English changed to some other language. It flowed! It didn't require any thought; it simply flowed from my lips. I had no clue what was going on!

I had never read about this, never spoke with anybody about this, hadn't seen this on television nor heard it on the radio or in church.

I thought I had simply lost my marbles! I had read this verse in the Gospels, but I did not apply it to this situation...

"The thief comes only to steal and kill and destroy" (Jo. 10:10 NIV).

Satan has access to our thought life. That's why we must combat his lies with the Word of God. Satan had a field day with me! "You have really lost your mind, Todd! This Christian stuff is driving you mad! Look at you... now you are making up silly words."

I didn't know at the time where these thoughts were coming from; it would be over a year later before I would understand that these were Satan's lies.

I did agree partly with what Satan was putting in my mind. I concluded that I was making up silly words, but I did not agree that this Christian stuff was driving me mad.

Fast forward seventeen months and I was discharged from the service and living back home with my parents. The experience I had driving my car and singing all those months ago vanished from my mind.

I had not lost my hunger for God's Word. During these

seventeen months I did a lot of reading in the Bible. I read a lot about the Holy Spirit. The more I read about the Holy Spirit the more I desired His work in my life. I read about the gift of speaking in tongues but that was not my focus. I never correlated speaking in tongues that I read in the Bible with the experience I had in my car.

I heard about two women who held a Bible study and emphasized the working of the Holy Spirit. I wanted to hear what they had to say. I didn't go to their Bible study, but I did call and make an appointment to meet with these two women. I shared my heart with them, and they wanted to pray over me. I had no problem with that. I remember that these two women prayed so fervently for me. They were coaching me to speak in tongues. Before I left, I encouraged them that everything was OK and for them not to be disappointed because it didn't go the way they wanted.

The next morning when I was taking a bath I was singing and praising the Lord as I would often do. Lo and behold while I was singing, my language changed, and I was praising the Lord "in the Spirit" and immediately the Lord brought back to my remembrance what happened a year and a half prior to this date. He spoke these words to my heart… "I gave you this gift a year and a half ago and because you didn't know what it was, the enemy easily convinced you that it wasn't real."

Over the past forty-nine years it has really disappointed me to witness the confusion and the distortion of understanding concerning the Holy Spirit. The Holy Spirit is such a precious part of the Trinity, God the Father, God the Son and God the Holy Spirit! The gifts of the Holy Spirit are just that… gifts! The gifts are not the Holy Spirit; they are just gifts *from* the Holy Spirit.

AN AMAZING JOURNEY

    Both of the following extremes are so damaging to people's understanding. One extreme says, "The Holy Spirit does not work that way anymore." The other extreme says, "If you don't speak in tongues, you don't have the Holy Spirit."

    This book is titled "An Amazing Journey" subtitled "Stones of Remembrance." There are plenty of theological books and commentaries with various viewpoints but that's not my intention with this book. This is a book about undeniable experiences I've had with the Lord Jesus Christ. I am simply sharing my heart about this "Amazing Journey."

7

Beginning Ministry and Marriage

"…God, who set me apart from birth and called me by his grace, was pleased to reveal his Son in me so that I might preach him…" (Gal. 1:15-16 NIV)

I embrace the above verse with all my heart. When my mom, out of desperation, tried a *self-induced* abortion God stepped in and did not allow it to happen. Millions have been called to preach Jesus; I'm just one of them. Can you only imagine how much we are loved and how much He wants to use each of us?

"God does not show favoritism" (Rom. 2:11 NIV).
Grasp this verse!
Who does God love more than you?
Not a single person.
How much does God want to use you?
Immeasurably!
What is God's ultimate purpose for you?
To glorify Him in whatever you do.

I knew there was a calling on my life before I was discharged out of the Coast Guard. A small church that I was attending during my final days in the military recognized my calling and gave me a *License to Preach* certificate on January 9, 1974.

AN AMAZING JOURNEY

I received my honorable discharge from the United States Coast Guard on July 19, 1974, and moved back to O'Fallon, Illinois. My dad was one of the superintendents building the St. Clair Square shopping mall in Fairview Heights, Illinois. He got me a job working as an apprentice carpenter, but it wasn't long before I wanted to go to college. I enrolled in the fall semester at McKendree College in Lebanon, Illinois in September of that same year. By the grace of God, the ADD and insecurities I experienced when I was younger were no longer there! I struggled through grade school and high school, now I was achieving As and Bs.

One morning I was sitting in church with my mom, listening to the pastor's Sunday message when the Holy Spirit spoke something so clearly to my heart and it was completely unrelated to the message. "I'm sending you to Carbondale, Illinois."

I was awestruck!

I took the Sunday bulletin and wrote a note to my mom... "Mom, the Lord just spoke to me and is sending me somewhere in the Carbondale area."

(Growing up in O'Fallon, we never used the term "southern Illinois." We would simply refer to southern Illinois as the "Carbondale area.")

I knew it. There was no doubt or question in my mind that this was God. I won't forget the look on my mother's face... "Are you sure?" I was so sure that I shared this with my pastor and sought his advice. This was a Methodist Church and the only reason I was going there was because it was my mother's church. I was still naïve to the doctrines of various churches, but at this time in my life it didn't matter.

Pastor Totten explained to me a little bit of the Methodist structure. To pastor a church in the Methodist organization I would be starting as a student pastor. I would have to receive a license to preach from the Methodist organization. This would require me going to their license-to-preach school. The primary goal of the school is to prepare the student for immediate pastoral leadership in a local church. Therefore, the school's educational direction is on practicality, and the studies are unapologetically a "crash course" on ministry in a local church.

I wanted to speak with someone about what the Lord said to me concerning a church somewhere in the Carbondale area. Pastor Totten advised me to speak with the District Superintendent (DS) that had jurisdiction over that area. I tried calling and could not get an answer but found his address, and since he lived in the same town where I went to college, I would simply make it a point to go by and visit with him.

This is another "never forget" scene…

I know he must have rolled his eyes when he saw what I did.

My zeal outweighed my tact. I allowed myself sufficient time to go by his house and share what was on my heart, and then still make it to class. He wasn't home, but I was not dissuaded. I took a piece of paper from my notebook and wrote a short message explaining how the Lord spoke to me about a church in the Carbondale area and left it between the main door and storm door. I wish I had a video recording of the look on his face when he saw the note. I left my contact information in the message but never heard back from him… no surprise.

I found out that the next license-to-preach school was being held in the Twin Cities of Champaign and Urbana, Illinois where the University of Illinois is located. The Methodist organization used classrooms in this university to conduct the two-week school.

What I did before I left for the university had great significance! I went to a local Christian bookstore looking for some

Christian material that I could take and read during these two weeks I would be gone. I can't remember if I bought anything, but I remember a young lady who captured my attention. We didn't speak, but she made a big impression on me. She was a beautiful girl with a radiant smile. As I left the bookstore, I was very impressed.

The two weeks at the license-to-preach school were life-changing! It wasn't the school, it's what happened at the school. One highlight was having the opportunity to preach to other young men and women who also had committed their lives to preach the gospel.

During my trip to the university, I sang, worshiped, and prayed while driving. As I was driving, I felt the Lord impress on my heart what I should preach at the school. I knew we would be preaching at some point during these two weeks. When the time came for my assignment to speak, I was greatly disappointed. We were given select verses that we had to use for our sermon. I thought "oh no!"... what if what the Lord has given me to share won't be in one of those verses? When I got back to my room and checked out these verses, my response was "Praise the Lord!" I could easily use these verses to speak what was on my heart.

The preaching was mainly for the purpose of critiquing, but I took this opportunity seriously. When would I ever again share with a room full of future pastors?

When my turn came, I began by sharing this...

"I know this is meant for critiquing, but I have something on my heart that the Lord spoke to me while I was driving here. My life has been radically changed by the power of God and each one of us here today has a responsibility before God in presenting the gospel unapologetically." I then continued with my message.

When a student was done with their sermon, the instructor would come up and critique our delivery. He emphasized that we needed three main points to work from, then each student was graded on whether they achieved those three points or not.

It was amazing what happened when I finished my sermon. Instead of the instructor doing what he usually did, he stood, looked at the class and said, "Before I grade this sermon, it needs our response." He asked the entire class to get on their knees and start praying. I was astonished at how the Holy Spirit moved on every heart in the room!

We had different classes with different instructors. This was the first time I had an eye-opening experience realizing the misconception of religion!

*"You should know this, Timothy, that in the last days there will be very difficult times… **They will act religious**, but they will reject the power that could make them godly. Stay away from people like that!" (2 Tim. 3:1-5 NLT)*

I had been devouring God's Word for the last two years and I was appalled at what I was hearing from some of the instructors. As I sat in class listening to unscriptural statements, I felt like I would explode if I didn't say something in defense of the gospel!

And… I did speak up!

I was not rude, but my stance became a thorn in the flesh to some of the instructors and some of the students. The boldness and confidence the Lord gave me was uncompromising. It would have been easier not to say anything, but my conscience would not let me remain silent.

A young lady came up to me towards the end of our two weeks and she said… "Todd, I had a difficult time with you when you first started disagreeing with some of the teachers. Now I really do respect you. Thank you for standing up for your convictions. You have been a positive influence on my life." She made everything I did worth it.

Before I share what happened next, I want to make something clear. I have never, and would never, seek God's guidance by randomly opening my Bible and then looking down at the first verse I see and taking that verse as an answer to prayer, however, this is the most profound thing that happened during those two weeks...

One evening I sat on my bed to do some Bible reading. I opened my Bible and when I looked down this verse jumped off the page...

"But from the beginning of creation, God MADE THEM MALE AND FEMALE. FOR THIS REASON, A MAN SHALL LEAVE HIS FATHER AND MOTHER, AND THE TWO SHALL BECOME ONE FLESH; so they are no longer two, but one flesh" (Mk. 10:6-8 NASB).

The above verse is taken from the New American Standard Bible. That's the version I was reading when I opened my Bible. The NASB capitalizes words in the New Testament that are quoted from the Old Testament. I did not capitalize the words in the above verse, that is exactly how it is written in the NASB.

Maybe the capitalization drew me to this verse, but as soon as I read this the Holy Spirit showed me something remarkable. Immediately, the young lady who worked in the bookstore visually came to my mind, and the Holy Spirit said, *"she will be your wife."*

Wow! What do you do with something like that? I was overwhelmed and left in a state of amazement!

Was this me? Was it God? Did I make it up? Had these two weeks of school affected me? This was profound!

I have already shared in previous chapters about the Holy Spirit speaking to me, but this was totally different. I immediately went to my knees. "Lord Jesus, did you really speak this to my heart?" I shared this with a good friend who was in the same class. He told me what I would have told someone else in a similar situation… "Oh Todd, you better be careful!"

I agreed.

You can only imagine what occupied my prayer time on the way home. The more I prayed, the more peace I had. I did not share this with anyone else, but I could not shake it.

Maybe you have the same question I had. How do I go home, go back to the bookstore, and tell this young lady that she is supposed to be my wife? I had not been home more than a day when I knew I had to do something. I drove out to the bookstore and sat in my car praying, "Lord, help me! I don't know how to do this." The Lord gave me peace and I walked inside. As I entered, I noticed this young lady was talking with two other ladies who also worked there. I detoured down one of the aisles praying for the Lord's intervention the whole time. Remarkably, which one of these ladies walked over to where I was and asked if she could help me? My future wife!

"May I help you?" she asked.

"If you only knew" was my thought!

Without wasting time, I told her my name and she told me that her name was Sue. I asked if I could take her out to dinner sometime. Her answer shocked me! "Yes, I would like that," but there was a hitch. She told me that her mom and dad were in Oklahoma at a camp meeting, and she was caring for her younger brother and sister until they returned."

I replied, "No problem, I've been asked to be a counselor at a youth camp for a week; I'll contact you when I get back."

Later I found out that Sue surprised herself when she heard

her voice agreeing to go out with me since she didn't know anything about me.

God was orchestrating everything. My purpose at youth camp was more than just being a counselor; He had prepared a man to give me good advice.

As I was getting settled in my sleeping quarters there was an older man in the barracks with me. We introduced ourselves and after some small talk he asked if I was married. "No" was my response.

He began to say… "Young man, I would like to give you some advice. When God brings the right person into your life you won't be 70% sure, you won't be 80% sure."

I'm thinking to myself, "Where is he going with this?"

He continued, "When God brings the right girl into your life you will be 100% sure."

Wow! This was a Divine appointment!

It had been nearly 2½ years since I gave my life to Jesus Christ. I had one date during this whole time. During this week of camp, I met three other young ladies who were friendly, and I enjoyed their company, but I could not get Sue out of my mind.

The day I got home I called Sue, "Is it okay if I come over and pick you up; we could get a soda, drive around and just talk?" She liked the idea. We had a wonderful time! After I took her home and was driving back, I could not hold back the tears. I knew right then that what God showed me was true. This was our first date.

In a few days I called Sue to set up our second date. She agreed, and we went to IHOP. We were having a great time visiting when I felt this nudging… "Ask her." Was this the Holy Spirit or Todd!? I sensed the Holy Spirit nudging me to share

Beginning Ministry and Marriage

with her the experience in the bookstore, and then what happened at the university when the Holy Spirit spoke to me that she would be my wife.

I do not know what was bigger, the lump in my throat or the beating of my heart! I politely excused myself and went to the restroom. I locked the door and began praying. "Lord Jesus, is this really you? I desperately need your help!" His still small voice spoke to my heart, "Trust me." When I went back to the table, I mustered up my faith and poured out my heart. I shared everything. Finally, I asked the question… "I am asking if… you will marry me?"

I was convinced that as miraculous as all of this was, surely the Holy Spirit was preparing her heart like he had mine. Boy, was I wrong! She did not have to say anything, her facial expression told it all. Sue was starting to go into shock! I jumped in with… "Please don't say anything!" I did not want to hear her say "No," so I stopped her before she had the chance.

What I did not know was that one year prior to this, Sue had been engaged and all the arrangements for a wedding were set. At the last minute she discovered serious problems with her fiancé that would have destroyed their marriage. Her heart was broken. She left Illinois for Oregon to stay with a friend–to be restored emotionally and spiritually. Now, one year later this man she barely knows asks her for marriage on their second date!

It becomes even more intense!

The next day I was painting trim on a house that I agreed to do for extra income. Here came the Holy Spirit's nudging again. This time I felt led to go over to Sue's house and speak with her mom! So, I did. The faith I was walking in was larger than normal. The Bible says…

"There are different kinds of spiritual gifts, but the same Spirit

is the source of them all… The same Spirit gives great faith to another…" (1 Cor. 12:4-9 NLT)

I would never have done it this way, but the Lord has His reasons, and I did not ask why. Sue was at work; I knocked on the door and Sue's mom was the only one home, and she invited me in. I shared everything just as I had shared with Sue. I did not expect to hear what she began telling me. When I asked Sue for a date at the bookstore, and she said that her mom and dad were away at a camp meeting in Oklahoma, this is what took place…

While at this meeting the Lord spoke to Shirley (Sue's mom). He said, "Sue will be married before the end of the year." Sue's mom and dad were people of faith, and God was working greatly in their lives. My story fascinated her.

I loved everything about Sue. We both decided to be patient and grow in our love and faith with each other. Clyde (Sue's dad) was a man of spiritual depth. When he looked at you, you could feel his eyes piercing into your innermost being. We all came to the same conclusion: if this was of God it would grow, if it wasn't, it would fade away. The four of us spent many evenings on the living room floor of their home praying for God's will to be accomplished. Our love and respect for each other (the four of us) was growing strong.

After Sue and I got married her dad and I became very close. Clyde was a tremendous man of God, and I had deep respect for him. He strongly supported our ministry.

I called the district superintendent to let him know that I'd completed the license-to-preach school, and that I was still interested in being a student pastor at a church located somewhere in the Carbondale area (southern Illinois). This was done with a phone call; we did not meet in person. He assured me that he would be looking for a church.

Beginning Ministry and Marriage

* * *

Sue and I met in July, and by August the Holy Spirit had put His seal of approval for marriage in our hearts. We loved to drive around, and we still do today. One afternoon we drove the river road alongside the Mississippi River to Pierre Marquette. I wanted to make this proposal special. I had her engagement ring in the glove box and asked if she would open the compartment door to get me something. She saw the small box, and her eyes welled up with tears, mine did also. When I asked her to marry me, her response was different from the first time!

We set the wedding date; it would be October 24th. I had no job, no income, but my faith had not wavered. I was the only one in the family who was not nervous. Shirley said generously, "If nothing else, we will let you live in our camper until you find a job." It was now September, and nothing had changed.

Not everyone was on board with this whirlwind engagement and marriage. I will never forget the day I shared this with my dad. He was outside working on a truck he was converting into a camper, and I shared my heart with him how the Lord had brought all this together. He was holding a tool in his hand which he slammed to the ground and said, "There is no way that you can meet this girl and after one date know that she is supposed to be your wife!"

I replied, "Dad, I know it goes against good reasoning, but I believe with all of my heart that this is the work of God."

After we did get married my dad loved Sue like a daughter!

My parents' phone rang, "Is Todd there? This is the Methodist District Superintendent whom Todd spoke with."

"Yes sir, this is Todd."

"Young man, you might find this hard to believe, but there is a church in southern Illinois looking for a student pastor, except there is a problem. They only want a student pastor who is married."

"No problem!" I said with excitement. "I'm getting married next month!"

On the morning of September 15, 1975, I loaded some clothes and books in my car and went down to a local store to buy a cot *(the parsonage did not have any furniture and we had not bought any yet)*. I arrived at the parsonage in Creal Springs to begin this ministry, and later that afternoon, a precious man by the name of "Shorty" Alsip stopped by to meet me. He noticed that there was no furniture, "Where is your furniture? Are you going to stay here like this?" he asked, almost in unbelief.

"I've got a cot; I'm good," and I meant it! Then he went home to get a mattress for me to use on the cot.

The next month, October 24, Sue and I were married. I enrolled at the University of SIU, Carbondale to continue my education to maintain my position as a student pastor.

Would I recommend this marriage technique for all couples? No, not without knowing for sure that you have heard from the Lord! In our case it has been wonderful! At the time of this writing Sue and I have been married for forty-six years and have been blessed with two children, one daughter-in-law and one granddaughter. We love each other deeply. We did not plan our marriage to begin the way it did, God did it! Remember, this is *An Amazing Journey!*

Our lives have been completely unscripted. What has not changed is an enduring faith that we have shared together from the first day we met.

The remaining chapters describe God's Divine Intervention in so many ways. We feel that our cup is full and running over!

8

Radio Waves Now Playing God's Tunes

"And whatever you do or say (even if you own a radio station), do it as a representative of the Lord Jesus..."
(Col. 3:17 NLT, words added within parentheses)

June 19, 1979, St. Louis Globe Democrat

MARION - While WKRP in Cincinnati shifted to an all-rock format in the fiction world of television, WGGH in Marion shifted from its all-rock to Christian message format in the real world of southern Illinois. "As far as I know, we are the only commercially-owned station in Illinois that has a Christian message format," George Dodds, owner and manager of the 5000 W station, said Monday.

Dodds went on to say, "Three years ago, a young Methodist minister came into the station and said he wanted to go on the air and talk about God." Dodds said he was hesitant but gave the minister 50 minutes on a Saturday afternoon. "I told him to use the personal pronoun you when talking to the people and not to ask for money throughout the broadcast." Dodds admitted he was a bit nervous when he first listened on that Saturday afternoon.

AN AMAZING JOURNEY

"I had instructed the man on the board (the engineer) if this gets too bad, cut him off and say the program was interrupted due to technical difficulties." But, as he listened, Dodds was impressed, a slow change had begun.

This all started in February 1976. I just finished class at SIU and needed to kill some time before my appointment with George Dodds at his radio station in Marion, Illinois. Mr. Dodds with his partner, Harley Grisham, built their radio station in 1949. They went on the air September 24. The idea of having a *Christian* radio station was not in the picture.

A pastor friend of mine had been discussing with me what would be involved in having a radio program. That intrigued me and I volunteered to find out. I called WGGH and set up an appointment with the owner and manager of the station. I had no personal interest in having a program, but the idea did spark some curiosity. I did not want to drive all the way back to Creal Springs only to turn around and drive back to Marion. A snack and a soft drink at McDonald's would be relaxing while I waited for the appointment.

I had nothing on my mind except enjoying my snack.

Then the still small voice of the Holy Spirit entered my thoughts! "You are meeting with Mr. Dodds, and this is what I want you to say! I want his radio station to be used for me in full-time Christian programming and I also have a program for you to conduct yourself."

I have heard this voice before; not often, but I knew it was the Holy Spirit! I was stunned. All my preplanned questions that I had for Mr. Dodds vanished. I had never met this man before, nor did I know anything about Mr. Dodds. I did not know if the Lord had been speaking to him about his station or not, but I became anxious about meeting this man.

Radio Waves Now Playing God's Tunes

I waited in the small lobby for someone to summon me to his office. It was not long before I was told he was ready to meet.

I began, "Mr. Dodds, my name is Todd Greiner and I appreciate this opportunity to meet with you." He was very gracious and kind without making me feel uncomfortable or rushed. I had prayed fervently during my drive from Carbondale to the station, for wisdom and for the Holy Spirit's leading. After talking for a few minutes Mr. Dodds asked about my purpose for the meeting.

"Mr. Dodds, do you believe that the Holy Spirit can speak to people?"

Mr. Dodds responded thoughtfully, "If you had asked me that question a year ago, I would have been skeptical, but in this last year I have witnessed many things that have convinced me otherwise."

"Mr. Dodds, I have something to share with you and I do it humbly and respectfully." I continued… "I actually was going to meet with you for another reason, but earlier today the Holy Spirit spoke to me about our meeting."

He didn't say anything, but his eyes and ears were at full attention! "Mr. Dodds, I know nothing about your station and I'm not familiar with your programming but when the Lord spoke to my heart, I was strongly impressed that He wants your station for full-time Christian programming."

He was amazed! "I have actually had thoughts along those lines," he replied. "I'm not saying what I will do, but I find the timing of this visit fascinating."

I needed the Lord to really help me with the next part of what I was about to ask. How do I come into this man's office and tell him the Lord wants me to have a program on his station? The Lord graciously humbled me. "Mr. Dodds, I have one more part of this I need to share."

AN AMAZING JOURNEY

Meet Todd Greiner! For over a year now, Todd has been challenging people's lives every Saturday afternoon on WGGH's "Reach Out". "Reach Out", which has just completed its first year on the air, began in February, 1976, and is heard each Saturday afternoon from 1:05 to 2:00 p.m. In Todd's own works, "Reach Out is a program showing in different people's lives the reality that Jesus Christ is the same yesterday, today and forever". "Reach Out" does not take a slant toward any denomination or religion, but simply presents a realistic look at the needs of the young and of the old.

Todd, originally form O'Fallon, Illinois, is 25 years old, married, and resides in Creal Springs. Todd said he was called by the Lord to come to Southern Illinois in 1975 for

George Dodds had this article put in the local newspaper three years after I started my program "Reach Out" (first half).

some reason, which turned out to be "Reach Out". If you have any doubts about what Jesus Christ can do today, listen to "Reach Out" and you'll find hope through the personal testimony of those who share their own personal experiences during the 55-minute program Todd interviews guests selected from various backgrounds, vocations, and walks of life, who all have a story to tell. For instance, a lady from Herrin had a muscle disease for over ten years and was instantly healed while praying for another. An area businessman who was losing his family because of his alcholoism, gave his life to Christ and was cured from alcoholism and his family was brought together again. A blind woman who started having epileptic seizures during her youth, shared how Jesus healed her from her seizures and blessed her with a very unique ministry in music. A local coal mine inspector shared the difference Jesus had made in his occupational work. A lady who had been involved with the syndicate, drugs and prostitution and had been pronounced dead by a doctor in a hospital bed, was brought back to life and her life was completely changed, in that she is now ministering the gospel of Jesus Christ. Todd invites each and everyone of you, whether you are a Christian or not, to tune in to "Reach Out"...a time you can be drawn to the simple sharing of each guest. Listen this Saturday at 1:05 p.m. to Tod Greiner and "Reach Out".

WGGH
ALL AMERICAN RADIO
5000 WATTS 1150 KHZ
MARION, ILL.

George Dodds had this article put in the local newspaper three years after I started my program "Reach Out" (second half).

"Okay," he reacted cautiously, "Mr. Dodds, I believe the Lord wants me to have a program."

"Tell me about it" he said.

As I began to share ideas about a program, I was amazed how thoughts were flowing into my mind as I spoke! To him it sounded like I had thought this all through, but I had not!

I continued… "What do you think if I had a one-hour program on Saturdays that would be used mainly for interviews with other Christians sharing testimonies of what God had done in their lives?"

"I like the idea," he answered. He concluded by saying, "Let me think about it."

George Dodds did convert the programming to a full-time Christian format. I kept my program called "Reach Out" for approximately four years. It was exciting to be a part of that transition. I felt humbled that God would use me to speak to the heart of George Dodds. I firmly believe that if God had not used me, He still would have accomplished His purpose by sending someone else.

In May 1991, station owner George W. Dodds, trading as Marion Broadcasting Company, reached an agreement to sell WGGH to Tri-State Christian TV, Inc.

The FCC dismissed this application on January 13, 1992.

In February 1992, Dodds reached a new sale agreement with Vine Broadcasting, Inc., and filed a new application with the FCC.

The FCC approved the transfer of the broadcast license on April 7, 1992, and the transaction was formally consummated on June 9, 1992. After this sale and more than 40 years of station ownership, Dodds retired from broadcasting.

9

The Real Sherlock Holmes

*"Let us think of ways to **motivate one another** to acts of love and good works. And let us not neglect our meeting together, as some people do, but **encourage one another**, especially now that the day of his return is drawing near"*
(Heb. 10:24,25 NLT).

Was Sherlock Holmes a real person? Sherlock Holmes is a fictional character created by the Scottish writer, Sir Arthur Conan Doyle. However, Conan Doyle did model Holmes's methods and mannerisms on those of Dr. Joseph Bell, who had been his professor at the University of Edinburgh Medical School.

I not only knew the real Sherlock Holmes, but I worked for him!

In 1976, I resigned my position as student pastor. I had no idea what the Lord had in store, but the decision to resign was no mistake. I resigned without having a job or money and our time in the parsonage was ending; we needed a home and a job soon!

We looked at renting with no success, and buying a house was not an option. There was a mobile home sales lot that we passed every day on our way into Marion. The name of the business was *Sherlock Holmes Mobile Homes*. We hadn't thought of living in a mobile home but, why not? We were impressed by how nice these homes were.

Sherlock had a very contagious smile!

The owner of the business was in fact Sherlock Holmes! His wife's name was Joan, and what wonderful people! They were using a mobile home for their office while an office/storage building was being built on location. They would be moving into their new office within a couple of weeks and said the mobile home they were using was for sale. Sue and I thought that the mobile home was perfect, and we wanted to apply for a loan.

We filled out the loan papers with Sherlock and he told us that he would contact us when the bank got back to him with a decision about the loan. However, we did not know what was going on behind the scenes. We had no idea how his business was set up. Only later did we discover that his sales requiring financing were based on the principle of recourse. In other words, *sales with recourse means liability for the asset sold falls upon the seller.*

The bank advised Sherlock that the loan was too much of

a risk. I had resigned my position at the church without a job awaiting me. We were newlyweds with little financial history. All I had for credit history was two car loans. Only later did we find out what Sherlock said… "I'm on recourse, I take full responsibility for the loan, and I feel good about this couple. I want to take the chance on giving them the loan."

Sue and I prayed about everything, and we were confident that a door would open where I was supposed to work. I put out many job applications. We were living in our new mobile home, and I still did not have a job.

I kept having this nagging thought… "Ask Sherlock for a job."

I did not doubt that a job would be available, but I did not like the idea of what I most likely would be doing. The idea of being a salesperson interested me, but I knew that Sherlock already had a salesperson, his name was Terrell Clark. I assumed that I would be part of the crew that sets up mobile homes. Why I resisted that idea I do not know. This was persistent for over a week. I remember the day I was about to break down in tears feeling such shame. I asked the Lord to forgive me of my pride in not asking Sherlock and Joan for a job.

I drove directly to the sales lot, walked into the office and told Joan that I wanted to speak with Sherlock.

She said, "Sherlock is out with a customer, can I help you?"

I responded, "Joan, I'm needing a job and I would love working for you and Sherlock."

"Are you serious?" she said enthusiastically while gazing over the top of her glasses. "Sherlock and I have been praying for another salesperson and the only person we've thought of is you!" Wow, God is awesome!

The Holy Spirit had been nudging me all this time to come

AN AMAZING JOURNEY

and ask for a job, and my pride kept getting in the way. This began an amazing new chapter in my life. Sherlock had recently made a deeper commitment to follow Jesus Christ. Joan was already a Christian. I knew without a doubt that the Lord had taken me from the small church I was pastoring, to personally encourage and help Sherlock spiritually!

We sold mobile and modular homes, but the work environment was quite different than most places. Consider the work environment that many people work in. Employees are often told "keep your religion at home." "Don't leave your Bible on your desk." "Don't pray publicly in this workplace." It was different at *Sherlock Holmes Mobile Homes!* Sherlock would confide in me, pray with me, and seek counsel and advice weekly. Sherlock and Joan loved Sue and I as if we were adopted children.

We had a large business sign on the property located right next to the highway, highly visible from both directions. It had the business logo plus a lighted message board. We would advertise special sales, etc. Sherlock decided that instead of promoting the business he wanted to promote the gospel by using the message board. I was usually the one who would change the sign. We would leave a message up a few weeks before changing it. He decided he wanted this message… "Be Sure and Worship This Sunday at the Church of Your Choice!"

After I put that message up it was not long before I had a visitor. I was by myself when this lady walked in and wanted to speak to the person responsible for the message.

"The owner of the business had me put that up," I answered with a smile.

Then she responded… "I am very offended by the message you put on your sign! I am Seventh-day Adventist and we do not worship on Sunday, the proper day to worship is on Saturday!"

Well, that was not what I was expected to hear. Remarkably, this verse popped immediately to mind…

"In the same way, some think one day is more holy than another day, while others think every day is alike. You should each be fully convinced that whichever day you choose is acceptable" (Rom. 14:5 NLT).

Without being disrespectful I shared this verse with her and said, "Ma'am you feel that one day is more holy than another day; I am in the group that thinks every day is special to God."

I smiled, and was hoping she would do the same, but she didn't. Then she left.

I was allowed to use the office to hold Bible studies and meet with people to give encouragement and counseling. Praying and talking about the Lord was never discouraged.

Sherlock had a heart of gold, but like most of us, he had a lot of rough edges that the Lord wanted to iron out. Those who knew him well knew that he had zero patience and was quick-tempered. When you work with someone six days a week it is not unusual to rub each other wrong at times. Amazingly, Sherlock and I had a great relationship. We loved each other and the whole time we worked together I don't remember a time when Sherlock was irritated with me. Not everyone who worked there could say the same.

Sherlock had three employees that did nothing but maintenance, warranty work and setting up the homes. They were often the target of his frustration. They were fired and rehired more than once. I remember one time that Sherlock got so mad he fired them all at the same time and the next day hired them all back!

Sherlock was very generous. You have heard it said that some people would give you the shirt off their back if you needed it? Sherlock really would. If you gave him the impression that he was being unfair or treating you wrong, it would light his fuse! Here is one perfect example…

We had sold a mobile home to a man that Sherlock worked with years earlier. By trade, Sherlock was a bricklayer and was excellent at it. Sherlock had given this man a large discount; it was a great deal. But the man didn't seem to appreciate it. Some people seem to be suspicious about everything, and he fit that category. After he had lived in his home for a while, he came back to the business to report a problem with his stove. Warranty work was a normal occurrence, so I took all the information and assured him that we would get someone to do the appliance warranty and that he had nothing to worry about; but that didn't seem to be convincing to him. I was by myself at the time, but he insisted that he must talk to Sherlock. I told him that if he didn't mind waiting a while it wouldn't be long before he returned.

I see this in my mind as if it happened yesterday.

Sherlock pulled up on the lot in his truck and got out. I didn't hear him, but I could tell by watching him that he was whistling a tune as he walked over to the office. This customer was sitting on the couch next to the door. Sherlock walked in smiling, said hello to me, then looked at his friend on the couch and said hello to him.

This is exactly what his friend said… "Sherlock, I thought I could trust you! My brand-new stove is a piece of junk!"

Oh my! Did this guy light Sherlock's fuse!

The smile on Sherlock's face vanished like a vapor. His face got red and then he lit into his friend. "What are you talking about?! Do you think I deliberately sold you a damaged stove? What's wrong with you?! If you want, I'll buy you a new one and gold plate the knobs!" Sherlock made his point!

His friend stood, put his hand over his heart and said… "Sherlock, I have a bad heart!"

With frustration Sherlock responded, "Take your bad heart and go home. We will do whatever we need to do next week to fix the problem!"

Later in the day Sherlock called his friend, apologized, and assured him that whatever the problem was it would be resolved, and for him not to worry about it.

He indeed had a heart of gold.

Sherlock loved his name. I'm sure when Sherlock's mom gave him his name she had a smile on her face, but Sherlock took advantage of it and knew how to use it. He had a twin sister named Shirley. Once he was pulled over for speeding and when the officer asked for his license and saw his name the officer chuckled and said, "You've got to be kidding!" and let him off without a ticket.

He loved to laugh, even at himself. I would go with him to mobile home dealer shows. Many manufacturers would represent their latest products. There was usually a lot of food around and we made it a point to visit all those places. He loved to give out his business cards with this statement… "I'm the real Sherlock Holmes and it's a pleasure to meet you!"

The Lord blessed Sherlock's business very much. He was a man of great integrity and those who knew him loved him.

The four years with Sherlock and Joan were a great blessing. I know without a doubt that the Lord sent me to Sherlock and Joan to help establish their relationship with Jesus Christ.

Around 1980, Sherlock sold the business to his lifetime best friend, J.B. Kuykendall and J.B.'s son-in-law, Ken Anderson. At the same time, I decided to become self-employed and sold underpinning and wood burners that were designed for mobile homes.

I had the honor to officiate both Joan and Sherlock's

memorial services when the Lord took them home. Joan departed this life in 2005, then Sherlock in 2020, Sherlock lived to be 93. In both services we celebrated their lives and the beautiful memories they left in the hearts of all who knew them.

10

One God-Encounter Will Change Everything

*"In the apostle Paul's day, people saw the transformation that had taken place in his life **after the encounter with the Lord** on the road to Damascus. His powerful testimony of what Christ had done in his life was riveting"* (Graham, Franklin. Through My Father's Eyes).

In 1977, while working for Sherlock, I had one of the most amazing experiences of my lifetime. It happened on Interstate 64 west of Mount Vernon, Illinois.

Sue's parents, who lived in Caseyville, Illinois would often drive down and visit. During one of those visits Sue agreed to take our son Matt, who was just a baby, and ride back with her parents to spend a few days with them. I'd drive up after work on Saturday to spend a short weekend, and the three of us would return home Sunday evening.

I worked six days a week at the sales lot from eight in the morning until it got dark. We did not have our model homes lit up so we wanted to take advantage of daylight hours as much as we could. Sherlock knew that I had plans to drive up to Caseyville after we closed on Saturday, so he was gracious

AN AMAZING JOURNEY

enough to allow me to leave early before normal quitting time. I worked long hours, so Sue and I treasured the time we could be together; as a result, I was anxious to get on the road. I had made this trip to Caseyville or O'Fallon during the last year many times. It was a routine drive with most of the trip being interstate driving that took approximately two hours.

I would take Interstate 57 from Marion to Mount Vernon, and then Interstate 64 to the Caseyville exit. When I got onto I-64 just outside of Mount Vernon there was approximately one hour of daylight left.

I was between 15 and 20 miles west of Mount Vernon when the Holy Spirit spoke to me vividly!

"You will see a car on the side of the road. Stop and help them."

I can hardly explain how I felt… anticipation, excitement, eagerness, and I did not have the slightest doubt that this would happen! My eyes were almost straining as I looked ahead as far as I could see. Would there actually be a car on the shoulder of the road? It seemed like 10 or 15 minutes, and lo and behold, I saw it! As I got closer, I also saw what looked like an older couple standing by the side of the car safely between the car and the ditch. With no hesitation I pulled over in front of their car then backed up closer to it.

I got out of my car and walked back to see what the problem was. As I approached them, I asked, "What's the problem, can I be of any help?"

With a worried look on his face the older gentleman replied, "We are in a difficult situation! We have a flat tire, and our spare tire's also flat." Then we introduced ourselves to each other.

Can you imagine how I felt right then?! Talk about mountain-moving faith, show me a mountain! This couple had a

One God-Encounter Will Change Everything

Ford car; I was driving a Chevy, but remember, my faith was ready to move a mountain!

I said, "Let me see if my spare will work on your car."

He responded, "Young man, I greatly appreciate you saying that, but are you not aware that we're driving two different manufactured cars and your Chevy rim will not fit this Ford?"

I was thinking maybe this is the mountain! "Let's try it anyway," I said with a touch of excitement. I could just envision the Lord making the Chevy lug bolt pattern match his Ford lug bolts!

You can't criticize childlike faith, right?

I got his jack out and jacked up the car so I could remove the wheel. I then took my spare out of the trunk and rolled it over to his car. Well, this is not the mountain the Lord had in mind! My lug bolt pattern on my spare tire did not match his lug bolts.

"No problem," I said.

His spare tire was not only flat but was not in good condition either. I did notice that my tire was the same size as his. So, without hesitancy I said, "Let's throw your tire and rim in my trunk along with my spare and I'm going to give you my spare tire and have it put on your rim." "I won't allow you to do that!" he said sternly.

"No sir, I insist!" I answered.

After loading both tires and rims in my trunk, we got in my car. He sat in the front seat and his wife sat in the back; it was now starting to get dark. I could tell they both were overwhelmed that this stranger would be willing to do this for them.

I was on my way to Okawville, a town not too far away that hopefully would have a service station able to do the tire change we needed. We hadn't been driving too long before this older man asked me a question… "Todd, what is that book on your dashboard?" I don't think he saw me place my Bible on the dashboard just prior to him getting in the car. It had been lying right where he would be sitting. "Sir," I passionately answered, "that is the greatest book that has ever been written since the beginning of time; it's my Bible." It got very quiet, then I heard whimpering coming from the lady in the backseat. After a few moments I asked, "Is everything okay?"

Then, with gentle sobbing, he spoke up, "Young man, you won't believe what has just happened! My wife and I have been seeking after God. Not ten minutes before you stopped, we prayed on the side of the road and asked the Lord, 'If you are real, please send somebody to help us,' we felt desperate, then we saw you pull over."

Glory to God, I just about came unglued!

I shared my side of the story how the Lord spoke to me around that same time, that I would see someone on the side of the road that needed help and I was to stop. We all three had an incredible encounter with the Lord Jesus Christ! We cried - we laughed - cried some more - and gave God all the glory! We marveled how in God's sovereignty He had put me on that highway at that appointed time and place, and while they were praying, he was speaking to my heart!

We did find a service station that was able to do the tire work we needed. He wanted to pay for the work and the tire, but I insisted that I would pay for it and give him my tire. I just experienced one of the greatest moments I have ever had in the Lord. How could I not pay for this?

For this St. Louis couple, the God-Encounter radically changed their lives. We had a brief mail exchange months after this experience. The Lord answered their prayer in a greater way than they ever expected. Not only did the Lord get them

One God-Encounter Will Change Everything

out of the distress of two bad tires, but He eternally changed their hearts. They shared that they were involved in a church and had volunteered for mission work.

Rarely can I pass that place on Interstate 64 without my heart leaping for joy, thanking the Lord for the privilege of being used on that beautiful Saturday afternoon.

11

For Everything There is a Season

"Your own ears will hear him. Right behind you a voice will say, "This is the way you should go…"
(Is. 30:21 NLT)

Seasonal changes are a great way to describe the different directions the Lord has taken Sue and me through our marriage. I stand firm on the truth that the Lord is always faithful, but not predictable. I love living in an area with different seasons. Fall is our favorite time of the year, but it would not be appreciated as much without the other seasons; I even enjoy the time change. This is a story about one of those profound seasonal changes.

When J.B. Kuykendall and his son-in-law, Ken Anderson, bought the mobile home business from Sherlock, I ventured out on my own, selling wood stoves and underpinning for mobile homes. I had been self-employed for less than a year when I was contacted by J.B. and asked if I would be willing to return to their business and be over the service department. It was a great opportunity, and I accepted the offer.

It was ironic that the work I was not wanting to do when I first asked Sherlock for a job, now became very enjoyable. J.B. subcontracted the setup of the homes to a company that was

For Everything There is a Season

independent of their own business. When one of their modular or mobile homes were set up, that's when I would come and complete the final trim work and utility hookups. Installing the air conditioning, electricity, plumbing and exterior siding was my responsibility. They bought me a new service van for work, and transportation to and from home.

I served as a fill-in pastor at a country church during most of this time, then Sue and I became involved with a church by the name of Community of Faith Church (COF), located in Carterville, Illinois. We loved the church and felt much at home. The pastor and I had a great friendship, and I assisted him in any way I could. I was asked if I would teach the adult Bible study and did so without any hesitation.

We were very content. I enjoyed the service work I was doing for Sherlock Holmes Mobile Homes; plus, the ministry I was doing at COF was gratifying. This arrangement lasted nearly two years. The great relationship I had with Sherlock Holmes continued with J.B. and Ken. I could not have worked for better people. I want to emphasize that I was not restless, discontented, or dissatisfied, but Sue and I never stopped crying out to the Lord for His will to be accomplished in our lives.

In the fall of 1982, another amazing event took place in our lives!

On a beautiful and peaceful fall morning as I was driving to work with nothing on my mind except thinking about the work I needed to do that day, the Spirit of God spoke something profound to my heart and mind!

"I want you to resign your job today. Tell J.B. and Ken that you will not leave them in a difficult position, but as of today you are resigning."

Wow! I did not see this coming! But I had no doubt that it was God.

No one had cell phones in those days, so I was not able to call Sue and check this out with her to see what she thought. When I got to work, I told J.B. and Ken that we needed to talk.

By the look on my face and the tone of my voice they knew I was serious. I loved these two men so much. I expressed my gratitude and appreciation for everything they had done for me and the love I had for them, then began to share my heart. I had never given them a hint of any dissatisfaction with my job. Both men loved Jesus Christ deeply. If it had not been for their own personal relationship with the Lord, they would have had a difficult time with what I shared. I told them what the Lord spoke to me and assured them that I would not leave them in a precarious situation, but to consider my resignation official that day.

They were stunned and surprised but neither of them looked at me as if I had lost my mind. They both respected my walk in the Lord, and I had never given them reason to think otherwise.

Sue knew nothing of this until I got home that night. "For Everything There Is a Season!"

Sue is an amazing person! Her love for the Lord and her love for me has never been questioned. She was not upset or worried; we both were excited to see what the Lord had next.

John Somers, the pastor of COF, and I had an appointment that evening to visit with a couple from the church. John picked me up at our house and we began visiting like we always did. It was not long before the typical question was asked by John, "How was your day, Todd? What have you been up to?"

I could not wait to share, "John, you won't believe it."

He could tell that I was excited… "Why, what happened?"

I continued, "John, the most amazing thing occurred this morning." I shared the whole story with him.

For Everything There is a Season

I can remember the very spot where we were in his car when John pulled off to the shoulder of the road in front of the Chevrolet dealership located on Highway 13 in Marion. We both could sense the strong presence of the Lord in the car.

Looking seriously at me he said, "Todd, you won't believe what I have to say!"

"Please, tell me," I responded.

John began sharing with me something that had been on his heart, and that he had been praying about for weeks. "Todd, I feel a great need to have an associate pastor. The only person that comes to my mind is you. I have not said anything because I knew you already had a job, and from what I could tell you were content with what you were doing. Since you have resigned what will you do now?"

"Wow, John, that is amazing!" I continued… "The Lord told me to resign and that's all He said. We have no idea if we will be moving or how He wants to use us, but we do have peace."

Intently he asked, "Would you consider being my associate pastor?" "John, I am open to anything, and being your associate pastor would be a great honor," I responded with tears.

He continued, "I will be leaving for a few days to attend a speaking engagement. Let's both be praying about this and when I get back, we'll get together and share how we feel the Lord is leading."

We did pray earnestly about this decision, and the Lord confirmed in both our hearts that this was indeed the direction He wanted.

How remarkable was this? On the day that the Lord spoke to my heart about resigning, that very evening I was asked to be the associate pastor for COF!

The transition from Sherlock Holmes Mobile Homes to

becoming the associate pastor was without a doubt the will of God. I continued to do service work for J.B. and Ken until they found a replacement, which didn't take long. Sue and I were already involved at COF, so the transition was very easy. The church was excited about the addition of an associate pastor.

12

The Anointing Is for More Than Preaching

"Then the LORD said to Moses, "Look, I have specifically chosen Bezalel son of Uri, grandson of Hur, of the tribe of Judah. **I have filled him with the Spirit of God, giving him great wisdom, ability, and expertise in all kinds of crafts"** *(Ex. 31:1-3 NLT).*

As Christians we talk about having a personal relationship with Jesus Christ, but what does that really mean? You cannot have a personal relationship with Jesus unless He has become your Lord and Savior. In the Lord's unique way, He took me on a journey revealing to me a personal relationship with Him in a way that I never knew. You can have salvation and still not understand the depth of the relationship He desires to have with all His children.

When the Lord used Moses to lead the Israelites out of Egypt it was an insurmountable task. The faith of the Israelites wavered like the surf of the sea and Moses was overwhelmed. Early in the journey Moses asked the Lord something very earnestly *"…You have told me, 'I know you by name, and I look favorably on you.' If it is true that you look favorably on me,* ***let***

AN AMAZING JOURNEY

me know your ways so I may understand you more fully *and continue to enjoy your favor"* (Ex. 33:12-13 NLT).

Moses entered a personal relationship with Almighty God that few have ever known. The more we understand His ways the more we will understand and know Him.

The Lord had blessed my time as associate pastor at COF, but I was becoming uneasy. Besides Pastor John, there were two associate pastors. Approximately one year after I became the associate pastor John decided to take on another associate pastor who would also serve as the worship leader. I know this was all part of God's plan. The uneasiness I felt came only from me. I like staying busy and felt like I was not busy enough.

When I resigned from working for J.B. and Ken, I had been doing some electrical troubleshooting and enjoyed it. Besides my love for ministering, I also had an interest in electrical work. If there was any electrical need at the church, I would always take care of it. There was a family in the church who was building a new facility for their business, so I went to John with this idea, "I would like to reach out to this family by wiring their building." It would be done for free since the church was taking care of my salary.

"Why not? That's a great idea" John replied. He continued, "If I need you for anything else you can drop what you're doing and then go back to it."

"Fantastic," I said.

I was still able to keep up with my responsibilities at the church in addition to doing the electrical wiring, and I loved it!

Then this verse kept coming to my mind…

"I have never coveted anyone's silver or gold or fine clothes. You know that ***these hands of mine have worked to supply my own needs…"*** *(Acts 20:33,34 NLT)*

I had a strong conviction to go back to self-employment

The Anointing Is for More Than Preaching

as an electrician and continue the ministry. When I presented this idea to John and the elders it was met with some opposition, but at the same time they could tell that my request was heartfelt, and they believed it could work. Most of what I was doing as an associate was teaching and assisting with counseling, so I was able to continue doing that along with my self-employment.

I relied strongly on the anointing of the Lord for preaching, teaching, counseling, and every ministry with which I was involved. Without His spirit we are powerless and ineffective. Unfortunately, this is how most of the church world understands the anointing of the Lord. They believe the anointing is for pastors, evangelists, missionaries, and every other ministry directly involved in His work. What about Christian doctors, lawyers, tradesmen, farmers, teachers, and every other reputable occupation?

"Whatever you do, work at it with all your heart, as working for the Lord, *not for men, since you know that you will receive an inheritance from the Lord as a reward.* ***It is the Lord Christ you are serving"*** *(Col. 3:23-24 NIV).*

Whatever work a Christian does, he or she does so unto the Lord! ***"It is the Lord Christ you are serving."***

The Lord not only wants to pour out His Spirit on those in ministry (as we understand ministry), but He wants to pour out His Spirit and anoint His children in whatever the occupation may be! We have done a disservice to the people of God in unconsciously promoting this idea that paid or full time ministry is the sole place for His anointing. I began the chapter with this verse...

"Then the LORD said to Moses, "Look, I have specifically chosen Bezalel son of Uri, grandson of Hur, of the tribe of Judah. ***I have filled him with the Spirit of God, giving him great***

AN AMAZING JOURNEY

wisdom, ability, and expertise in all kinds of crafts" (Ex. 31:1-3 NLT).

If Bezalel had not been filled with the Holy Spirit of God, it would have been impossible for him to carry out the mission of building the tabernacle with the skill and expertise he had.

I was overcome with the realization that the Holy Spirit wanted to anoint and teach me how to be an electrician as much as He wanted to anoint me in the pulpit!

The church world has unintentionally painted a picture that full-time ministry is more spiritual than what we call "bi-vocational "ministry. This is how Google sees it...

"A bi-vocational ("dual-occupation") pastor is usually shepherding a church of smaller size or serving in an area with a depressed economy. The fact that his congregation is unable to provide him a living wage is what forces him to be a bi-vocational pastor. The call to the ministry is still there, and the pastor heeds the call; it's just that practical concerns, such as putting food on the table, require him to take a second job and serve the congregation as a bi-vocational pastor."

The apostle Paul was bi-vocational as a tent maker. He was extremely grateful to the churches who periodically gave him support so he didn't have to continue working as much with his hands and ministering at the same time. However, when you read the book of Acts the Lord's anointing upon him was just as strong whether he was working as a tent maker or not.

When I made the decision to work full time as a self-employed electrician, I needed the Lord's hand upon me just as strong as any time in my life. I did not go through the Brotherhood of Electrical Workers as an apprentice. My initial experience with any electrical work came when I worked for Sherlock Holmes Mobile Homes. It's amazing how quickly a person can learn something when it's accompanied by a strong

The Anointing Is for More Than Preaching

passion; that's exactly what I had. I was devouring electrical books and the electrical code. I could not go out on my own as a self-employed electrician without certification. I took the same electrical test that any electrician would take to become licensed and completed it successfully. The Lord blessed my business. It was during this time that I discovered how much the Lord wanted to be involved with me just as much as if I were in a "full-time ministry."

I had contractors that would give me their new construction projects. I did old house rewiring and some commercial work. The Lord's favor was with me in all that I did. Countless times if I was facing something challenging, I would lift my voice to the Lord for His wisdom and understanding and He always worked it out. I was never apprehensive or hesitant in asking for advice. The manager of Marion Electric, Dennis Brewer, was a great help many times.

I had a friend who was in the ministry and bi-vocational. He struggled with guilt and condemnation, feeling that his "secular work" was unspiritual and un-gratifying. It was sad to see him struggle with this which led to such discouragement.

I'm very thankful for that time in my life which taught me so much about the working of the Holy Spirit and His anointing upon my life whether I was standing behind the pulpit preaching God's Word or rewiring an old house!

13

Brought Full-Circle by Divine Appointment

Someone has said "We come full circle when we experience a series of developments or circumstances that lead us back to the original source, position, or situation. It kind of feels like déjà vu but with a twist."

In a previous chapter I shared about an amazing event that took place in the fall of 1982. The same day that the Lord spoke to me about resigning my position at Sherlock Holmes Mobile Homes, I was asked by Pastor John Somers if I would be his associate pastor, and I accepted the position.

I was his associate pastor for approximately two years before I became a self-employed licensed electrician. About four years into my electrical business J.B. Kuykendall asked me if I would return to Sherlock Holmes Mobile Homes as a salesman. I had enjoyed working with J.B. so much in the past, and he presented a good proposal. So, I agreed and completed the projects that I had already been committed to without accepting any new ones.

While doing my electrical business I also served as an elder at Community Faith Church (COF).

Brought Full-Circle by Divine Appointment

In the fall of 1988, I had a very strong impression of something that I couldn't shake. I shared this with one of the other elders and I assured him that no one had said anything to me, including Pastor John. I felt firmly that Pastor John would be resigning. When I shared this with the elder his expression was one of complete disbelief. The church was doing well, and John had been the only senior pastor since the conception of the church nine years earlier. I told this elder not to share this with anyone, but just make it a matter of prayer.

Then it happened!

We would meet once a month as elders with the pastor. It had been less than a month since I shared with this elder about Pastor John. At the close of our meeting in late fall Pastor John said, "Men, I need to share with you what the Lord has put on my heart." He shared with us that he would be resigning and starting a church in Carbondale and wanted to ask the people in the church who lived close to the Carbondale area to join him in this new work. All of us were stunned, including me! The elder whom I confided in looked over at me with an open jaw. Even though I had felt this so strongly, it still came as a great surprise. I didn't know what I was expecting, but this wasn't quite it.

Then John went on to share how he believed that I should serve as interim pastor until they would find a replacement for him. He did say that he did not believe that I should be the pastor, but to serve only temporarily until they found a replacement. We were all greatly surprised. John asked me if I was okay with his suggestion, and I replied by saying, "We will definitely make it a matter of prayer."

John was a highly respected pastor, and everybody loved him. When he shared this with the entire church it was also received with disbelief and sadness.

AN AMAZING JOURNEY

* * *

A night to remember!

There were five men in the church who served as elders: Don, CD, Sherlock, Tony, and me. (Two of these elders have already gone on to be with the Lord, including Pastor John). Tony invited the other four elders over to his house so we could discuss the situation and pray together as a group.

They asked me how I felt about serving as an interim pastor. I told them I would do it under one condition. I stipulated that I wanted all of us to meet, not once a month, but weekly for prayer. We would seek the Lord for every decision we made including finding the replacement for John and for the grace I needed to serve as interim pastor. They all agreed, and we decided to start seeking the Lord that very evening. Not one of those elders have forgotten what happened that night... the glory of God descended upon us! We would do everything we could to support John's wishes with zero criticism, whether we agreed with what he was doing or not. I had gone through my own seasonal changes through life; there was no allowance for criticism!

On January 1, 1989, I officially became the senior pastor of COF on an interim basis. After one year the elders decided something needed to be done with the title "interim." I never said a word about it. They never interviewed anyone else for the position. They decided it needed to be brought to a vote before the congregation; the only input I gave was that I wanted the vote to be at least 80% in favor of me being their permanent pastor. The vote was taken and all I knew was that I was still their pastor; they never told me how the vote turned out.

14

The Refuge Home

Definition of a refuge: shelter or protection from danger or distress; a place that provides shelter or protection; something to which one has recourse in difficulty.

"No, I don't want you to buy this property; move your mobile home to the church property and I also want you to build a home that will be used for ministry." I was stunned! I knew that these words had come from the Lord.

These are the events that led up to hearing this word from the Lord…

The year was 1994 and our family lived in a mobile home in a rural area just outside a small village called Spillertown, Illinois. We owned the mobile home and rented the lot space. The gentleman who owned the lot that we were renting had four rental spaces for mobile homes. The area was well-kept. We had developed a good relationship with the landlord and his wife. After living there for a while, we were curious whether the landlord would be willing to sell the lot we were renting plus the lot in front of ours. It was a pretty area in a good location, and we thought it would be a good idea to buy these two lots.

AN AMAZING JOURNEY

When I discussed my offer with the landlord, he was hesitant. The property had been in his family for many years and the idea of selling was something he'd never considered. He did say that we would be great neighbors and he would be willing to think it over. After a couple weeks he met with me and said he would rather not sell at this time. I told him that I completely understood.

Sue and I have always trusted the Lord to either open a door or close a door, according to His will, so we had peace about the closing of that door and just laid it down.

A few months went by and there was a knock on our door; it was our landlord. He asked if we could talk, and I invited him inside. What he said really blessed my heart, "Todd, Lydia and I think so much of you and Sue, and we've given a lot of thought to the idea of selling these two lots, and if you still want to buy them, we are willing to sell." We were blessed by his response.

Sue and I still wanted to buy the property, so I went to a local bank to apply for a loan. Everything looked good and I was told that I would be contacted in approximately a week with their decision. Sure enough, it was about one week when I got a phone call... "Todd, everything looks good, the loan has been approved and you can come to the bank to sign papers and pick up the check at your convenience."

God's timing is perfect whether we think so or not! I never went to the bank! It was not long after receiving the call from the bank that I heard these words...

"No, I don't want you to buy this property. Move your mobile home to the church property and I also want you to build a home that will be used for ministry." I was stunned! I knew that these words had come from the Lord.

Sue and I had learned over the years not to question the leadership of the Holy Spirit!

The Refuge Home

These thoughts came to Sue and me, but we did not entertain them...

"Lord, why didn't I know this before applying for the loan?"

"Lord, why didn't I know this before talking to the landlord?"

The landlord and the bank were both gracious. I thanked the bank for approving the loan and shared with them how we had changed our mind. It was hard for me to go to the landlord and share this because I was the one who originally put the thought in their minds about our desire to buy the property. Our landlord and his wife were both Christians and loved the Lord very much. I shared the whole story and even though they were surprised, they had a lot of respect for Sue and me and respected our decision with no hurt feelings.

The one person who was having the most difficulty with this was Sue.

The idea of moving our home to the church property was difficult for her to accept.

I had a close relationship with the church elders and knew I had to share this with them. I wouldn't dare take it upon myself to have our mobile home moved to the church property on my own! I shared the whole story with the elders, and they were amazed at what God had done.

However, they had two legitimate questions...

When do you plan to move your home out here, and how will the home that we are to build be used for ministry?

I loved those elders so much! They knew and believed that God worked outside the box!

As far as answering these two questions with the elders, this is what I said... "The answer to these questions will only come as we bathe all of this in a lot of prayer." I had been learning

AN AMAZING JOURNEY

more and more over the years how to recognize the voice of the Lord, and I knew that this was the Lord speaking to my heart.

My biggest concern now was Sue. I knew that the Lord was not going to put us in a situation that would cause division or stress. I assured Sue that we would not rush anything and that we would wait until she had peace and if she never received the peace, we would drop the idea. I never brought the subject up, and never made her feel bad about her decision.

One year later…

Sue came to me and said, "Honey, we need to talk."

Sue opened her heart and shared how the Lord had been dealing with her. She shared how the Lord had completely changed her attitude about moving out to the church. One year prior to this, the idea of taking our mobile home out to the church property was intimidating. In her words, "I'd feel like I was living in a fishbowl."

I went a year, leaving it in the Lord's hands, believing that if it was His will He would change Sue's heart, and He did.

Even though God had not revealed the whole plan yet, it was time to obey and take a leap of faith! I shared this with the elders at our next meeting and said I was ready to make the move. We had made this a matter of prayer throughout the year, and everyone felt it was God's will to proceed. The church had nineteen acres of property, and approximately four acres were woods.

We began by clearing just enough of the woods for our mobile home. Utilities had to be put in and moving our home went quicker and easier than we had imagined. Sue and I both had total peace about living on the church property.

Now it was time to focus on the other part of what God spoke to me. What kind of home did the Lord want us to build and for what purpose?

The Refuge Home

This had been a major prayer concern for the last year leading up to this time. We were a church that took a strong stand for the life of the unborn. Every few weeks a large group of us would go up to Granite City, Illinois to do a peaceful protest at the abortion clinic. Because of our strong stand against abortion, the elders and I believed that this home we'd build would in some way be used to minister to young women who were pregnant and had made the decision to keep their babies. Building this home was not something known only to the leadership of the church. I brought this to the attention of the entire church that we all needed to be praying for God's guidance as we moved forward to whatever it was the Lord wanted us to do.

I contacted a woman named Carla who was the director of a facility located in Mount Vernon, Illinois. This facility was specifically used for young women who were pregnant and needed a place to live until the time of their delivery. If needed, they could extend their stay long enough to find other housing. We did not want to reinvent the wheel, so any advice Carla could give us was greatly appreciated.

The elders and I went as a group to meet with Carla. She was gracious and spent considerable time talking with us, answering questions and giving advice. Before we left, she got very serious and opened her heart, asking if she could be totally honest with us.

"Of course!" I replied.

"Gentlemen, to be completely honest I want to share with you something I feel strongly about." Again, I encouraged her to please do so. "I don't believe southern Illinois is needing another facility like ours. We are not the only facility that will house a pregnant girl while she's carrying her baby. The problem we have is having a place for the women to go *after* the baby is born."

AN AMAZING JOURNEY

Carla was completely amazed at our response… The elders and I looked at each other and said, "That's it!" The Lord confirmed to each one of us at that moment that this was indeed what He wanted us to do! For the last year we had been seeking the Lord in prayer for exactly what He wanted us to do… This was it!

When Carla saw how we responded to what she shared she was almost in tears. She was overwhelmed that we would decide that quickly. Truthfully, it wasn't as quick as she thought because it had been a matter of prayer for much longer than she knew.

I shared with the church how the Lord had brought clarity and direction to what we were to do, and the church was excited!

It did not take long for us to come up with plans for what we would call "The Refuge Home." One of the elders had a background in architectural design and all the planning was done "in-house."

We set a date to have a groundbreaking service after church on Sunday, July 30, 1995. I believe the entire church stayed for the groundbreaking service except for a few that had no choice. I shared this verse with the group…

"Unless the LORD builds the house, its builders labor in vain" (Ps. 127:1 NIV).

We had a large circle of people around the area where the Refuge Home would be built. We had worship, prayer and poured anointing oil on the ground; joy filled our hearts!

The church was debt-free, and we did not borrow any money for the construction of The Refuge Home. The work was mostly done by people within the church body. The

The Refuge Home

construction of the home went well, and we had an open house in January 1997.

The home was designed to house six women and their babies. Each woman had her own bedroom and two rooms shared one bathroom. There was an apartment for the house parents, and another room for the relief house parents that would come in on the weekends.

The daily operation of The Refuge Home required many volunteers who were committed to the challenges of this type of ministry. Besides having a full-time director, the home also required houseparents who lived in the home. The volunteers would start early in the morning and work until 4:00 pm. at which time the houseparents would be on full-time duty until the next morning. There were relief houseparents who were also volunteers that would come in on the weekends to give the full-time houseparents time off.

It was quite an adventure in our trust in the Lord because none of us had ever been involved with this type of ministry before. The result was amazing. Other than normal challenges that would be expected, the daily operation was a witness to God's amazing grace. All the glory goes to God, and I personally applaud every volunteer for their tremendous work!

The mothers were allowed to live in the home as long as necessary to receive schooling at a local college, training as a single parent, and the skills necessary to raise their child. Another book could be written following the lives of these young women after their time in The Refuge Home.

The Refuge Home was a tremendous ministry that gave much-needed help to these young women at a time in their lives when the need was so great. We knew of no other facility in the area that was being used for a similar purpose.

By the grace of God, thirty-five young mothers and

thirty-six babies (one set of twins) were given the opportunity to have a new start in their lives. As of this writing we know that two of the babies who previously lived in The Refuge Home are now attending Southern Illinois University, and both are honor students.

15

Expose It!

"Have nothing to do with the fruitless deeds of darkness, but rather expose them" (Eph. 5:11 NIV).

Wednesday, April 11, 2007, I received a phone call from a lady in our church that would exemplify the beginning of a radical shift in the direction our church would take for the next two years.

"Todd, are you aware of what's happening with the Marion High School?" "No," I responded bewildered.

Laurie went on to say, "I'm surprised you don't know. The Marion High School is involved in a lawsuit; it's awful!"

"Please, what's it about?"

Laurie continued, "This lawsuit originated due to an evangelist who was holding meetings in a local church. He was invited to the school to deliver a secular anti-drug/alcohol speech to the students."

"Did he preach to the kids?" I asked.

Laurie made this very clear. "No, not at all. Some kids who went to the church he was speaking at invited their friends and were handing out pizza coupons for free pizza if anybody wanted to come. That was the extent of it." Laurie went on to add the following… "Todd, the school administrators are full of fear and have decided that at the graduation no prayers will be allowed!"

This had me troubled.

Every Thursday morning the men in our church would meet for prayer from 6:00 a.m. to 7:00 a.m. The timing was perfect; I had just spoken with Laurie the day before and this matter was still weighing on my heart. We were careful in using our prayer time effectively, and at 6:00 a.m. we promptly began praying. This morning would be slightly different. When it looked like everyone was there, I stood and shared my heart. "Men, there is something very serious that we need to pray about this morning." I shared the details with them.

Taking turns praying, we spent almost the entire hour praying specifically for what was going on at the high school; crying out that God would intervene powerfully!

After our prayer time we usually would go to a local McDonald's for coffee and breakfast. As we were talking, sharing, and enjoying our breakfast, the Holy Spirit spoke to me in an unbelievable way! This is what He said…

"I want you to take out a full-page ad in the newspaper and expose what's been done." I knew immediately that this was the Holy Spirit! I quickly spoke up, "Men, the Lord has just spoken to me about what we should do!"

They were immediately curious.

"The Lord has made it clear to me that we are to take out a full-page ad in The Southern Illinoisan and expose the lawsuit." We had never done anything like this before! As surprised as each one of us were, no one questioned that it came from God.

When I got back to my office, I decided to call the District Superintendent of Schools. I waited until I thought he would be in his office and made the call. After introducing myself I asked about the lawsuit. He said, "We have been instructed not to bring up the subject, but since you're asking and I'm not the one bringing it up, I'll give you the details."

He shared the whole story. When I told him about the full-page ad, he couldn't believe it. I also asked him to please get me all the exact figures and exact details. The last thing I wanted to do was put in print something that was not accurate! He said he would work on it and get the information to me as soon as he could.

I had never taken out a full-page ad in the paper before and was naïve about the procedure.

I called The Southern Illinoisan newspaper and said that I wanted to take out an ad. After being transferred to the proper person I stated what I wanted to do. I wanted the ad to come out the next day, Friday. This is when my naïveté really showed up! "I'm sorry sir, you have to schedule in advance a full-page ad, there's no way that we could do this tomorrow."

I was devastated! *(There was a reason why the ad needed to come out the next day, because the following Tuesday would be an election for the Marion School Board, about which I will explain more later).* She continued… "I don't see any way we could do this but give me a few minutes and I'll be right back."

I waited what seemed to be a long time and then she got back on the phone. "Sir… you won't believe this! There has been a cancellation on a full-page ad that was scheduled to come out tomorrow. We can do it!" Wow, God was aware of this when He spoke to my heart!

The next thing she said caught me off guard… "Todd, we need to have all the information brought in before 2:00 p.m. in order to meet the deadline for tomorrow's paper." My naïveté shows up again! I'm not sure what I was thinking but having everything ready by that time seemed overwhelming.

AN AMAZING JOURNEY

Asking my staff to meet me in my office right away, I explained the situation and asked that we would all pray for the ability to get this done in time. After we were done praying, I still felt overwhelmed. I decided that I would call The Southern Illinoisan and see if we could postpone until Saturday or Monday.

I called The Southern Illinoisan and explained that I didn't think I would be able to meet their deadline. The lady I had been working with wanted this ad to run because I had previously explained to her our intentions. She said, "Don't worry about the 2:00 p.m. deadline; we will make it work! Bring in what you have, and I will help lay it out for you." This was amazing!

Later, I received a phone call from the high school with the information necessary to complete the ad. I gathered all the information I had and went to the newspaper office. The lady who was working with me was very helpful and did an excellent job laying out the ad.

OUTRAGED!

The Marion School District's tort immunity fund (funded by our tax dollars) has spent to date $167,328.61 in defense of the lawsuit filed by   (of Marion) against the Marion Community Unit School District Number 2.

This lawsuit originated because   (who was holding evangelical meetings in a local church) **DELIVERED A SECULAR ANTI-DRUG/ALCOHOL SPEECH TO STUDENTS.**

The ad was full-page, this is only the top part which was very eye-catching.

Expose It!

The complaint went into detail to allege that the school district was endorsing religion by permitting the evangelist to speak to the students. The judge dismissed the case earlier in the year citing a lack of evidence that any of the allegations had merit. The plaintiff filed a motion for reconsideration of the judge's ruling and asked for additional time for discovery. He cited that there was new evidence that the school district had violated the establishment clause of the U.S. Constitution by allowing an invocation to be given by a student at graduation. The plaintiff's complaint was that the prayer was evangelical and mentioned Jesus's name. The judge did not allow this new evidence in the case but left open the door for a new lawsuit on this issue. The case was transferred to a new judge and placed under reconsideration.

It was imperative to me that the ad come out Friday because the election would be held on the following Tuesday for seats on the Marion school board. What brought even more concern was that the plaintiff's wife was running for one of the seats on the board. Five individuals were running for one of four seats available. The odds of winning one of the seats was high.

The ad did not reflect any bias on who should be voted for. This is the information that was on the bottom of the ad...

The majority of citizens of Southern Illinois who are aware of this are outraged by this allegation!
Dr. ----- (wife of -----) is now running for a seat on the Marion School Board! Citizens of Marion should be aware of this when voting in the School Board election Tuesday, April 17.

AN AMAZING JOURNEY

The following day, Friday, April 13, 2007, the full-page ad appeared in The Southern Illinoisan. It looked amazing and the message was powerful!

I had scheduled spending the day with a friend who was an Illinois State Trooper, Rob Reynolds. I'd signed a waiver allowing me to ride in his state police car and observe what a day in his life is like. I had done this once before and found it interesting.

At approximately 9:00 a.m. in the morning I received a call from Diane, the church secretary. She was in tears; she had just received a call from someone threatening to sue our church for the ad in the paper. The call was disturbing, and remarks were made, leaving Diane troubled. I felt terrible that she had to receive the call and talk to this person instead of me dealing with it. I told her that I would have Rob take me back to the church and assured her that I would intercept any other calls like this.

There were many other phone calls throughout the day, but this is how they usually went...

"Is this the church that put the ad in the paper about the high school lawsuit?" Cautiously, Diane would answer with a hesitant yes. "Thank you! We appreciate your church having the boldness to do this!"

Out of all the phone calls received that day regarding the ad, all of them were positive except for the first one, and we were confident we knew who that came from.

Interestingly, something very remarkable happened at the end of the day. I was still in my office when I heard a knock on the door. It was Carl, our custodian, telling me that there was someone who wanted to speak with me. Reminded of that first phone call, I didn't think this would go well... but I was wrong. It happened to be a local businessman I knew. He did not attend our church and he had a serious look on his face when he asked how much we paid for the ad. His tone of voice made me somewhat hesitant to tell him, but I did... "The cost of the ad was $2000."

He immediately answered, "The Lord told me to come over here and pay for it."

I replied, "Wow, well then it was actually a little less than $2000!"

With a big smile on his face he said, "I'll go ahead and make the check for $2000."

The following day after the ad debuted, the plaintiffs obviously wanted a rebuttal. On the front page of The Southern Illinoisan the main headline read...

MARION SCHOOL BOARD CANDIDATE EXPLAINS LAWSUIT

To quote the plaintiff's wife who was running for a seat on the school board... "I am disappointed that some Marion residents are up in arms about my candidacy for the Marion Unit 2 School Board because of the lawsuit."

Then she shot herself in the foot, to quote...

"Should she win the election Tuesday, she has worked it out with her husband to **drop the lawsuit**, perhaps paving the way for a more amicable relationship with the superintendent and board members."

One of the definitions for blackmail: *to force or coerce into a particular action.* In other words, "If you vote for me, we will consider dropping the lawsuit."

The following Wednesday, the morning after the election, the plaintiffs once again appeared in The Southern Illinoisan. She had lost by a landslide, quoting the paper... "She was a considerable distance behind fourth-place finisher—2,909 votes."

AN AMAZING JOURNEY

* * *

I had no idea what would transpire when I heard the voice of the Lord speak to my heart about putting the full-page ad in the paper! It ignited a fire in the hearts of many of the students at the Marion High School. They were overwhelmed that a local church would take a bold stand for them and for their rights. They had been squelched by fear and intimidation but now they felt revived. This was witnessed at the graduation. Remember, they had been told there would be no prayer during the graduation ceremony.

The seniors had preplanned what they would do at the graduation. The valedictorian gave the signal and one of the students stood up and started reciting the Lord's prayer. As he was doing this, other students stood to their feet and joined in. It spread like fire… Parents, grandparents, friends, and guests all stood up and joined in. The board members on the platform joined in until finally the whole audience was reciting the Lord's prayer to the glory of God!

The plaintiffs who filed a lawsuit against the school also filed against our church for putting the ad in the paper. They had no grounds because nothing inflammatory was said. The ad did not endorse anyone running for a seat on the school board; it was only informational, and the lawsuit came to nothing.

What did we learn? A lot!

I need to go back a few years to explain this. For a long time, my spirit had been troubled. Did Jesus Christ go to the cross, suffer and die, just so we would "Go to church?" I believe with all my heart that Christianity in America today is suffering. We have reduced Christianity to a mindset that if we just attend a church on a regular basis that's all God really wants from us. This mindset had been troubling me for years.

Jesus said that His church would be the salt of the earth and the light of the world…

"***You are the salt of the earth***. *But if the salt loses its saltiness, how can it be made salty again? It is no longer good for anything, except to be thrown out and trampled by men.* ***You are the light of the world***. *A city on a hill cannot be hidden. Neither do people light a lamp and put it under a bowl. Instead they put it on its stand, and it gives light to everyone in the house. In the same way, let your light shine before men, that they may see your good deeds and praise your Father in heaven*" (Mat. 5:13-16 NIV).

This can be summed up in five words…

ARE WE INFLUENCING THE WORLD?

This experience with the ad in the paper made a dynamic change in my heart and in my vision. If we maintain the "Go to Church" mentality we will never be the influence that Jesus wants.

The Church is the bride of Christ and is very precious to Him. Instead, the church has become self-seeking, self-gratifying, seeking entertainment. We should be influencing the world towards Jesus Christ and His kingdom!

Placing the ad in the paper had more influence than a multitude of sermons. When the high school students took a bold stand and recited the Lord's prayer it touched the heart of God and influenced the community.

After this experience the Lord spoke to my heart again and said… *"This is not the last time you will be using the paper for my purpose."*

16

Baby Samuel

"For you created my inmost being; you knit me together in my mother's womb. I praise you because I am fearfully and wonderfully made; your works are wonderful, I know that full well" (Ps. 139:13-14 NIV).

A LESSON FROM SAMUEL
A CHILD OR A CHOICE?

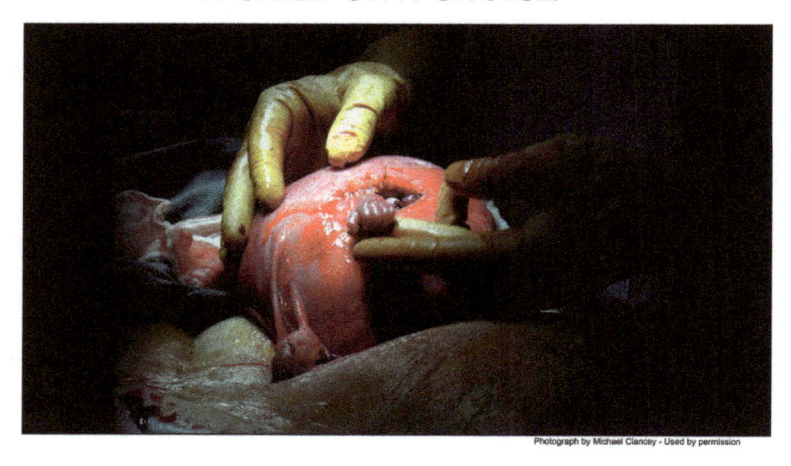

Photograph by Michael Clancey - Used by permission

Baby Samuel reaching his hand through the opening of the uterus and squeezing the doctor's finger.

Baby Samuel

Community of Faith Church took a strong stand for the life of the unborn. It's easy to "talk the talk" but the real question is do we "walk the talk?" Building the Refuge Home was a test to see if we were serious about what we said we believed. The Refuge Home proved to be a great blessing and gave many young women a chance for a new start with the responsibility of having a baby.

Little did we know that we were getting ready for another big test!

I had come across a picture that left me awestruck. The picture at the start of this chapter was taken by Michael Clancy, a veteran photojournalist from Nashville, Tennessee. He had been hired by USA Today newspaper to photograph a spina bifida corrective surgical procedure. You've heard the phrase "A picture is worth a thousand words," this picture was priceless! A thousand words would still be inadequate. The battle over the "viability" of the fetus is always raging. When a woman is pregnant is she carrying a glob of tissue, or a living baby? This picture virtually shuts the door on the argument. As the surgery was being performed, the baby's hand reached through the opening of the uterus and squeezed the doctor's finger! This picture went viral! Not just through the United States, but around the world.

I was on a mission; I had to find this photographer. I was able to find contact information and sent an email. He graciously responded and we had a great dialogue. I asked if we could use his picture for a full-page ad in The Southern Illinoisan. He asked for no compensation and said that he would be honored if we would use his picture. All he asked was that we would send him a copy of the ad. Little did we both know that this conversation would lead to a great friendship.

AN AMAZING JOURNEY

EVERY UNBORN CHILD DESERVES A CHANCE AT LIFE

Samuel is a precious living baby inside his mother's womb. The word "fetus" literally means "unborn offspring." Today, many people think a fetus is nothing more than an unformed mass without shape or feelings. This type of thinking makes it easier for a young mother, with an unplanned pregnancy, to consider abortion. Samuel is a living human being with feelings, a heart beat, and a future; and has as much right to life as anyone!

This was the bottom portion of the ad.

The Southern Illinoisan was happy to print the ad as it was, with no changes. They had no problem with the colored image. The full-page ad appeared Friday, May 11, 2007, and the response from the community was positive.

Michael Clancy wrote a book entitled *Hand of Hope, The Story Behind The Picture.* The book describes in detail all that led up to the taking of the picture and the events that followed. You could not imagine how one picture would have such a dramatic impact for the life of the unborn.

Michael devoted one chapter to his experience in coming to Community Faith Church. I have reprinted this chapter with his permission. The following is his chapter thirteen.

"I received an email from Todd Greiner, the Pastor of Community of Faith Church in Carterville, Illinois. He wanted to use the picture in a full-page ad in their local newspaper, the Southern Illinoisian. I sent him a file of the picture and their ad published May 11, 2007. Pastor Todd sent me a copy and it looked fantastic. One morning I was awakened by the familiar ping of newly arrived email. The TV show "House" recreated my picture in an episode called "Fetal Position." It

Baby Samuel

aired the night before. I'd never seen the show, but it was exciting to receive the email from those that had.

Wow, things are happening. God is at work. Pastor Todd emailed again on June 22, 2007. This time his congregation wanted to publish the same ad in USA Today. The cost for them would be, his word, "astronomical." Over the next couple of months, he worked with the ad department at USA Today. They claimed the picture was too graphic. This was unbelievable considering I shot the picture for them. They published it in full color for their story about spina bifida. The picture was changed to black and white and still it was considered too graphic.

Pastor Todd joked with me, "Maybe I could get more publicity if I called Sean Hannity and told him that USA Today refused to run our ad." He made several more submissions and the final image was almost unrecognizable from the original picture. The ad published on August 6, 2007, on page 5 of the "A" section, for a fee of $75,000. Jeff Johnson, with American Family Radio Network, contacted me and asked if I would do an interview August 7, 2007. It lasted for 25 minutes.

Pastor Todd called and said, "Michael, you need a few days of R & R. Would you consider driving up for a visit next weekend and sharing your story with our congregation? Sue and I have a few acres with a pond and it's very private."

"Absolutely," I said. I realized as I drove, I would be stepping up to the podium on August 19, 2007. The eighth anniversary of taking the picture. The drive was a little over three hours. Pastor Todd asked me if I would take a walk with him. "It's gorgeous here, Todd, you are blessed," I said.

"God gave me something to say to you, Michael. Do not let man steal your joy." Tears welled up in my eyes because that is exactly what I'd done. I allowed the doctor's denial of the picture to destroy my joy.

We had a relaxing weekend, and I shared my story with his congregation on Sunday morning. After the service, Pastor Todd and I went into his office, and he handed me an envelope.

"Should I open it?" I asked.

"Yes," he replied. It was a check for $9,500! "Todd, I can't take this," I said. "You don't have a choice," he replied. "Our congregation took up a collection for you." I couldn't help it; I cried, uncontrollably. Pastor Todd, Sue and I met several members of his church at a restaurant for lunch. Afterward, we said our goodbyes. I cried most of the way home, and thanked God for blessing me.

I prayed about what to do with the money. I ordered a small, extremely powerful projector I could take to events and created a presentation in Keynote. I had a VHS tape of Samuel and me testifying before the Senate hearing. I converted it to digital and included several clips in my new presentation. I also bought a remote control to advance my slides. Now, I would be able to deliver a powerful presentation with my speech.

I shared my story at ten events the last three months of 2007. On September 22, 2007, I spoke at the 34th Annual Right to Life of Michigan Affiliate Conference in Lansing. A gentleman, Dr. Daniel J. Pepin, came up immediately after I left the podium and said, "Don't ever get good at telling that story." I was crushed. Then, I realized what he meant. I was not a polished speaker and that's what made my story have such an impact. Each event left me emotionally and physically drained."

Putting a full-page color ad of "Baby Samuel" in the USA Today newspaper tested me and our congregation both spiritually and financially.

Being led by the Holy Spirit is the most precious experience

Baby Samuel

known to man. I have heard people pray, "Lord, do whatever it takes for me to hear your voice even if you have to hit me with a baseball bat!" The Lord does not want to hit you or me with a baseball bat, or use any other extreme measure for us to hear His voice…

"Do not be like the horse or the mule, which have no understanding but must be controlled by bit and bridle or they will not come to you" (Ps. 32:9 NIV).

I love these passages in 1 Kings when the Lord spoke to Elijah…

"And the word of the LORD came to him: "What are you doing here, Elijah?" …The LORD said, "Go out and stand on the mountain in the presence of the LORD, for the LORD is about to pass by." Then a great and powerful wind tore the mountains apart and shattered the rocks before the LORD, **but the LORD was not in the wind**. *After the wind there was an earthquake,* **but the LORD was not in the earthquake**. *After the earthquake came a fire,* **but the LORD was not in the fire**. *And after the fire came a* **gentle whisper**. *When* **Elijah heard it**, *he pulled his cloak over his face and went out and stood at the mouth of the cave" (1 Ki. 19:9-13 NIV).*

Throughout my lifetime I have been learning that the Lord does not want to lead me with a bit and bridle or a strong wind, earthquake, or a fire but He wants me to listen to the gentle whisper of the Holy Spirit.

It was His gentle whisper that spoke to my heart about putting another full-page ad in the newspaper but not a local newspaper. It was the USA Today!

When I shared this idea with the elders I was so blessed and encouraged with their openness and faith to trust God in whatever He was leading us to do. "Let's pray and see if God confirms this idea in all of our hearts before we make our next move" was their response. At this time, we had no idea what the cost would be. What was so beautiful was the fact that we were not counting the cost to determine if it was God's will, but to see if God confirmed the idea in our hearts first. The Lord did confirm in our hearts that it was His will to proceed, so it was time to find out the cost.

I contacted the USA Today and was connected with a representative who would walk us through the project. We wanted to do a full-page color ad just like we had done with the Southern Illinoisan. A onetime full-page color ad would cost us $150,000! (This is why I made this statement earlier in the chapter… "Little did we know that we were getting ready for another huge test!")

Were we shocked? Yes! Were we discouraged? No!

The elders and I believed this was the will of God and now I needed to bring this before the church.

Like most churches, our membership and our average weekly attendance was quite different. We had an approximate membership of over 700 people and an average attendance of about 450. We were a large church for our area but not that big of church to take on a project like this. How was the church going to respond to a financial mission like this?

I did not hesitate in bringing this before the church. I remember it clearly like it happened yesterday. I shared that the Lord was leading us to put another full-page ad in the paper and everyone responded positively. I said that the Lord was leading us to put a full-page ad of "Baby Samuel" in the USA Today. The response was applause! After quieting the people down, I shared that they may not want to clap when I tell them what it was going to cost… $150,000.

After a few moments of shock, the applause returned!

Now came the second half of this momentous mission.

Baby Samuel

We needed to raise the money in two weeks. The congregation slowly clapped again. The Lord had given the church a supernatural measure of faith!

Our church did not have a surplus of funds. We believed that what the Lord gave us financially was not meant to be placed in savings but to be used in kingdom work! We were blessed with the physical structures of our church and did everything necessary for upkeep and maintenance but had no ambition to build bigger and better.

The money that flowed in during the next two weeks was astonishing. Our church had never made such financial sacrifices as what was being done during the raising of this money. One lady in our church whose name was Teri, took money that they had set aside for doing some remodeling in their home and gave it for this mission! Bradley was another individual who took his coin collection he had been saving since childhood and donated it to this mission believing it was worthy to do so.

Sacrifices like this were made by many people. Several people were not even waiting for the two weeks but would come to the church office and write a check for this special offering.

The day of the offering will be a day that I will never forget! Plans had already been made for a small group to count the offering before the church service ended so the people could know exactly if we met our goal. I had instructed our church secretary to bring a note to me at the end of the service and present it to me with an unemotional expression. How she did this I'll never know!

Even as I'm writing this, my emotions are deeply stirred with praise and thanksgiving. To this day I have never experienced anything to this magnitude. Diane walked up to the pulpit and handed me the note with her unemotional expression.

I took the note, opened it, and smiled. That's all it took for a spontaneous eruption of genuine praise! I didn't say how much we collected; I only smiled. People across the congregation started standing, lifting hands, and shouting praises to the Lord! To my amazement, this literally continued for minutes.

When I read aloud the amount that was collected, the applause and praise erupted again! We exceeded the $150,000 we had hoped to collect.

God had miraculously given us the money, but now an unexpected roadblock developed.

When I sent the picture and information for the ad, the USA Today rejected it! Unbelievable! They were the ones who originally sent Michael Clancy on an assignment to take this picture and write the article. USA Today put the color picture in the paper after it was first taken, now they said it's too graphic. The representative who was working with me was very helpful, but the upper-level executives did not approve of the graphic nature of the photo.

If the full-page color ad had been approved, the cost would have been $150,000. Now they said we would have to go with black and white; that was good and bad. We wanted the picture like it had been in the Southern Illinoisan which was in color. A black and white picture would not be as impactful as color, so that would not be good, but the upside was that it would cost $75,000. We first tried the exact same picture, changing it to black and white, and that was denied. We were starting to get discouraged but we felt that the Lord did not want us to quit. We finally agreed on a black and white blowup of the hand with the other part of the picture eliminated. The graphics were not the same, but the message did not change so we agreed to proceed.

Baby Samuel

* * *

The ad came out on Monday, August 6, 2007, all across America and other parts of the world where the USA Today is sent. We sent copies of the ad to Dr. James Dobson of Focus on the Family. He kindly replied with an encouraging letter…

8605 EXPLORER DR., COLORADO SPRINGS, CO 80920 • 719-531-3400 • FAMILY.ORG

November 1, 2007

Pastor Todd Greiner
Community of Faith Church
1105 North Refuge Road
Carterville, IL 62918-9451

Dear Pastor Greiner:

Greetings from Focus on the Family, and many thanks for your very kind letter, accompanied by copies of the *USA Today* ads that were recently sponsored by your church. How encouraging to see such courageous, unflinching support for the pro-life cause! Your resolve not to cast any vote for a candidate who advances abortion is especially meaningful to me. At a time when I'm taking many hits for my perspective on the upcoming elections, it's heartening to hear from friends like you who share my conviction that we must not compromise on the essential moral issues of our time. To do so would be disastrous for our culture, and my conscience simply will not allow me to yield on matters that are laid out so clearly and unequivocally in Scripture. Let's continue praying that the Lord will guide our nation through an election season that, I believe, will be one of the most pivotal we've ever faced.

Thanks again for writing, Pastor Greiner. I value your support for me and for the ministry of Focus, and I applaud the sacrifices made by your church family to issue statements that firmly proclaim the value of life in the womb. Please extend my heartfelt appreciation to your congregation for me, won't you? God's richest blessings to everyone at Community of Faith Church in the days ahead!

Sincerely,

James C. Dobson, Ph.D.
Founder and Chairman

Dr. James Dobson responds to our ad placed in the USA Today

The $150,000 we collected in those two weeks was specifically for the purpose of advancing the fight for the unborn. Even though we had only spent half of it on the "Baby Samuel" ad, the remaining $75,000 was going to be used for the same purpose.

We created a second ad entitled "The American Dream" which came out September 24, 2007.

These numbers were current in September, 2007… The ad stated, "Since 1973, 48,589,993 United States citizens have been deprived of the American dream!"

IS IT POSSIBLE THAT THE PERSON WHO WOULD HAVE…

… Discovered the cure for cancer never had the chance?

… Discovered the cure for AIDS never had the chance?

… Discovered the path to peace in the Middle East never had the chance?

… Discovered an economical and efficient source of energy never had the chance?

ABORTION DESTROYS THE AMERICAN DREAM!

This was not the last full-page ad that we would put in a newspaper. Jesus told us the following…

"You are the salt of the earth. But if the salt loses its saltiness, how can it be made salty again? It is no longer good for anything, except to be thrown out and trampled by men. "You are the light of the world. A city on a hill cannot be hidden. Neither do people light a lamp and put it under a bowl. Instead, they put it on its stand, and it gives light to everyone in the house. In the same way, let your light shine before men, that they may see your good deeds and praise your Father in heaven" (Mat. 5:13-16 NIV).

To sum up what Jesus was saying in a few words is this… The church *(Christians)* should have a dynamic influence in this world! The silence of the church is not golden. The church should be speaking in the political realm and other areas of influence to bring the purpose and will of God into everyday life. Michael Clancy's picture of "Baby Samuel" was used in a powerful way in advancing the rights of the unborn. I was extremely thankful that our church had a heart to see this done. Collecting $150,000 for two full-page ads in the USA Today was outstanding!

17

The Church Needs a Bus

"And my God will meet all your needs according to his glorious riches in Christ Jesus" (Phil. 4:19 NIV).

What a tremendous work of God! This is not a story of benevolence, but an amazing story of supernatural provision by the Lord God Almighty!

The Lord was nudging my heart about purchasing a bus for our church *(Whiteash Freewill Baptist Church)*. We prayed about it often. One morning after Sue and I had been praying about this, Sue said, "Honey, don't you think it would be a good idea to check with the pastor first to see if they would even want a bus?" "Yes, that certainly makes good sense." So, I set up an appointment to meet with Pastor Andy.

I asked Andy if they ever thought about purchasing a bus or even had a need for one.

"Yes, many times, he responded. "We've prayed about this often and have looked at a couple of buses, but they were not in very good condition." I asked Andy what he thought I meant by a "bus." We both had different thoughts about what type of bus we needed. In my mind I had envisioned a large, commercial touring bus. Andy was thinking more in line with a shuttle. I shared my reasons why I thought a large touring bus would be

The Church Needs a Bus

more appropriate for our church. I could envision the bus for ministry outreach; in addition, passenger capacity and overall comfort outweighed what we could accomplish with a shuttle. I simply shared my heart with Andy about all of this without making any commitment.

Andy wanted to bounce these thoughts off someone else, which I'm glad he did. He spoke with another person in the church whom he highly respected, especially in matters like this. This person agreed with my reasoning.

It might seem simple to receive a gift like a bus, but what about maintenance, insurance, protective shelter, etc.? These would become the responsibility of the church.

Years earlier, I pastored a church, and we purchased an MCI bus which worked perfectly for the needs of our church. It was fantastic to see how this bus opened many opportunities of ministry we would not have had otherwise. Dave Maragni was our youth pastor at the time, and he had a genuine heart for outreach. He read in the paper about a young boy who was killed during a shooting at Cabrini Green in Chicago. He wrote the school a letter and offered to come to the school and minister encouragement to the students and teachers if they so desired. They wrote back, not only to thank him, but to take him up on his offer and invited him to their school. It was amazing how the Lord opened the door for our church to continue going up yearly, and sometimes twice a year ministering to the students and faculty. Without the bus we could not have accomplished this.

Another gentleman in our church at that time, Virgil Holderfield, got connected with some people at Pine Ridge Indian Reservation in South Dakota, not far from Wounded Knee. This was another door the Lord opened for a much-needed ministry that would not have happened had we not had appropriate transportation. We made many trips to Chicago and South Dakota along with other trips ministering in the name of the Lord Jesus.

Considering these past experiences, I desired to find another MCI bus and began doing a lot of research on what make/model and type of bus would be best and where to locate it. It's not as easy as it sounds. None of this was being done without much prayer. As a matter of fact, it was amazing how the Lord was showing us how to pray. It was more than just praying for a bus; it was praying for the bus He wanted us to have! We truly believed if He wanted us to have a bus, He would provide one that would be best for our church, in the greatest overall condition.

As this story progresses you will see the Divine Intervention of the Lord.

I called MCI's main office in Des Plains, Illinois, and left a message with the man who was head of sales over the Midwest region. I explained what I wanted to do, the reason for it and my phone number. I expected a call back soon, which I never received, but this was all part of God's plan that I didn't know at the time.

Yes, I was disappointed; however, we were praying and trusting the Lord to open or close any doors He wanted. Maybe the bus idea was my idea, not His!

A friend of mine has a large trucking business and I asked his advice on where I might be able to track down a good bus. He told me about a source they use when trying to find a specific truck and recommended that I use the same source. I did; I checked on two or three buses, but nothing fit our criteria.

I began thinking MCI never received the voicemail that I left at their office, so I called and left another one. It had already been approximately two weeks since the first voicemail.

The Church Needs a Bus

We continued praying and I continued searching. "Lord, is this something you really want us to do?"

Approximately one week after leaving the second voicemail I received a voicemail on my phone. It was from a gentleman named Bob who was head of sales at MCI over the Midwest region. He apologized and explained that when he received the first voicemail, he made a note, placed it on his desk, and it got covered up with other papers. When he received the second voicemail, he had full intention of getting right back to me and got sidetracked. I had no problem accepting that because I've been guilty of that myself. This was Divine Intervention that neither one of us realized at the time.

I called Bob back and explained what I was looking for, and that it would be given to a church. Getting a new bus was never a consideration! The type of bus I was looking for in a new model was $550,000. I told him that we would be willing to spend approximately $65,000 on a good used bus. He said that we probably could find a good used bus in the $65,000 to $70,000 price range. *(I am only sharing numbers because it is necessary to see the Divine Hand of God in the development of this story!)*

A few days later Bob called me back and said that he had found exactly what we were looking for. I was excited! They had taken in two buses that belonged to a touring business located in Michigan. They both were priced the same amount, $70,000. He'd talked with his boss and explained what the bus was going to be used for and they were willing to sell either bus for $60,000! That sounded great! I asked Bob to please check out the undercarriage for extensive rust, any damage on the vehicle, interior, engine, and basically making sure it was in good overall condition. He emailed me spec sheets on each bus.

I shared all this with Pastor Andy. Andy had been checking

with the finance committee and the trustees to see if they would be willing to take on the responsibility of having a bus, and they asked if I would be willing to meet with them. I told him I would be happy to.

The meeting was set, and I had the privilege to meet with these men. I shared everything and brought copies of the spec sheets on the two buses that Bob had told me about. I was honest about what God had put in my heart and shared some personal preferences.

I said, "Men I'll be honest, I'm willing to do this with some strings attached. After the purchase of the bus, the church resumes all financial responsibility." I also stated that I was willing to do more than just offer the bus, I also wanted to offer my experience as a qualified driver. I had driven thousands of miles in a bus and understood the enormous responsibility of owning one. I later found out that if I had not shared that I was willing to take oversight of the bus, they would have been reluctant moving forward with the responsibility of ownership. They would be praying about it and talk with the finance committee.

Within two or three days I got another call from Bob. He said, "Todd, I can't sell you either one of those buses." I was not disappointed; I was thankful! Not because I didn't want to purchase one of the buses, but because of his honesty in thoroughly checking each of them out. I enthusiastically thanked him. He said since these buses came from Michigan, and with all the snow and salt on the roads, the undercarriage was very rusty. Wow! That's the kind of man I want to work with! He told me that the head salesman in California was receiving some buses and one of them might work perfect for what we wanted. I was open to the idea.

During this time, I continued doing research on the MCI

buses to be aware of any problems that needed to be identified before we would make this purchase. I found out that the EPA regulations in 2007 required all diesel trucks to use what's called DEF fluid. That stands for "Diesel Exhaust Fluid." The initial requirement of this change caused major malfunctions with the engine. I did not want to purchase a bus that required DEF!

I received another call from Bob. I could tell that our relationship was becoming more than just business. We had a genuine respect for each other. He said, "Todd, I found your bus! It's in California; there are *two* buses to choose from. They both are 2007 models."

"Oh no!" I explained that I did not want a DEF bus. He said, "No worries." Both buses are 2007 models with 2006 engines. MCI knew what they would be facing, and at the time purchased an extra stock of 2006 engines to put in their new 2007 buses. Neither one of these buses were DEF models!

Bob gave me contact information for the head sales representative with MCI on the West Coast. Their office was in Los Alamitos, California. The gentleman to whom I was referred was named Marshall. Bob had already told Marshall everything I was looking for in a bus. When I spoke with Marshall, we really clicked with each other, he was a genuine Christian which blessed my heart so much! Between the two buses, Marshall highly recommended one and sent me information about it. The bus was listed for $75,000.

They needed to sell these buses as quickly as they could and were willing to discount this bus to $50,000! I was ecstatic! But it was conditional… I needed to come out to California and bring the bus back myself; there would be no delivery of the bus. Not a problem! I would enjoy the 2000-mile trip and look forward to it.

AN AMAZING JOURNEY

I asked if they would put a backup camera on the bus and they agreed to do it at an additional cost. "No problem," I said, "please put it on." They wanted the cost of the backup camera and installation paid upfront and mailed, which I did. I was to bring with me a $50,000 cashier's check when I arrived in California. A date was set for me to fly out to get the bus. I invited Mark Schwarm, a very good friend, to go to California with me to pick up the bus. Mark did not have credentials to drive the bus back but going 2,000 miles in this unfamiliar bus by myself was not the smartest thing to do. If I got into a situation in which I needed an extra pair of eyes, or someone outside the bus to guide with parking or maneuvering, it would be smart to have help.

Meanwhile, I was checking with a service facility located in Anna, Illinois, to see if they would be willing to do maintenance on the bus after I brought it back. I own a promotional advertising business and they were clients, as well as friends. The two owners are Gerald and Silas. I was telling Silas about the bus and gave him information how to find the bus on the Internet.

The next day Silas called me back. "Todd, I did find your bus and it was listed for $35,000, correct?" I responded "What?! What price did you say?" Silas said, "$35,000." I couldn't believe what I heard. I received what I thought was a tremendous discount from a $75,000 bus, down to $50,000! Surely there was a major mistake somewhere!

I called Bob at the Des Plains office. I said "Bob, I trust and respect you, but I found conflicting information that has me puzzled." I explained to him what Silas had told me and he too was shocked and in disbelief! He said, "Todd, let me make some calls and I'll get back with you as soon as I can."

It was between three to four hours later when he finally

called me back. These were his words… "Todd, you are the recipient of a $15,000 gift on top of the other major discounts you've already received."

There were two buses in California that were both priced at $75,000. One of the buses had engine issues that needed to be corrected and they lowered the price of that bus to $35,000. When Silas went on the Internet, he found the bus with the engine issues, *not* the bus we wanted to purchase.

Bob went on to explain that as he researched these buses, he discovered a mistake had been made. Instead of just lowering the price of the bus with engine issues, they accidentally lowered the price on *both* buses to $35,000! And because it was advertised for $35,000, they had to honor that price. I was overwhelmed with gratitude! Bob said, "Todd, it was our fault and though I'm not happy about the mistake, I'm actually glad it is going to you and to your church."

The story gets better!

Earlier in the story I mentioned that the delay in Bob getting back to me was God's Divine Intervention… now I can explain it.

This part of the story *(explained below)* was not realized until I reached California. Mark and I arrived early in the morning at Orange County Airport in California. Marshall picked us up and then we drove to Los Alamitos. We were not going to drive the bus back to Illinois until the next day, so, we had the entire day to spend with Marshall and go completely through the bus. It was not until then that we realized the Divine Intervention of the Lord in the process of purchasing this bus!…

Earlier in this story I explained how I did not want a DEF required bus. We arrived in California on Veterans Day which was November 11. In less than two months California would be enforcing a new law that would have a major impact on bus sales and other diesel truck sales. All diesel-powered trucks could no longer be registered in the state of California starting January 1, 2020, unless they were DEF equipped! This meant that the bus we were purchasing could no longer be registered in the state of California in approximately 45 days from the day we arrived. When they made the mistake in advertising the bus for $35,000, they could have reneged on that and insisted that it was their mistake, and they would hold firm on the price they needed to get for the bus. Bob told me that they would honor what they did because it was their mistake and I do believe that, but there was more incentive to sell the bus to us at $35,000! The delay in Bob originally getting back to me set in motion these events which allowed us to be enormously blessed with a $75,000 bus for $35,000!

I have shared numerical values in the story only because it was necessary to understand the full impact of what God did in his Divine plan with this bus.

The Lord Almighty laid His hand on this bus deal! He was not done!

The bus needed to have a title transfer, be registered, and license plates ordered. I had been told to expect the license plates to cost over $1,000. "If that needs to be, so be it," I thought.

Due to a misunderstanding, we were not able to get these items accomplished at the first DMV office. Pastor Andy was with me and neither one of us were pleased with the way things were being done. We waited a few days and I asked Andy if he would try again to go back to that same office and get these documents taken care of. He responded with, "Todd, why don't you go to the smaller DMV that's located in Benton and see if you get better service?" I agreed.

As the representative from the DMV worked with me, I

The Church Needs a Bus

explained that the bus was not going to be used for any commercial transportation but, for church purposes only.

She said, "I understand," then showed me the breakdown of pricing for the license plates. The gross vehicle weight of our bus is 54,000 pounds, which meant, the cost of our license plates would be $1,649 each year. I had been told to expect the cost to be over $1,000 but, before I signed any pa pers and wrote a check, I asked, "Is there anyone else in the office who might know a little bit more about this to see if our church would get any kind of discount on these plates?"

She kindly responded, "As a matter of fact, there is a lady that has worked here in the office for over 35 years and is very knowledgeable about all these things."

"May I please speak with her?" I asked.

This lady was God sent! If I had not asked for help from anyone else, I could have easily paid the $1,649. This other lady, with all her experience, looked everything over carefully. She said, "Let me go check something and I'll be right back." She came back with a smile on her face and said, "I did find something you qualify for." I was hoping for a few hundred dollars discounted. The cost of the license plates was reduced from $1,649 to be paid yearly, to $10 paid every two years!

I shared this story because it is all part of the "Amazing Journey." The intervention of God in financial matters has been very distorted in modern Christian teaching, but God cares about all our needs and blesses in ways we could never imagine.

18

Barbara

"In the same way, let your light shine before men, that they may see your good deeds and praise your Father in heaven" (Mat. 5:16 NIV).

Why do we do good deeds? To be noticed, applauded, receive thanks, to gain a reputation of being a generous and kind person? Or do we pray that whatever we do would be done in such a way that the person we are doing it for knows that it came from the Lord, and we were only an instrument?

My mom came from a large family; she was the youngest of eleven children—nine girls and two boys. With a family that large I couldn't tell you how many cousins I have. Her two brothers lived in St. Louis. One of her brothers had five children, four girls and one boy. Out of all my relatives I was closest to this family. The three oldest girls and I were close in age. I still maintain a close relationship with two of these girls; I love them like sisters. One of them is named Barbara.

Barb was having triple bypass surgery in July 2021 which is a serious surgery. Sue and I kept her in our prayers, knowing this would be a tough time. Barb is a realtor and lives alone. Not only would the recovery be hard, but she would not be able to show houses, and being a realtor was her only source of income.

Barbara

The Lord used Sue and me to show His love for her in a way that was evident and deeply touched her heart. To understand the impact of what He did, it's important to see her heart. Sue and I love Barb very much and I wanted to include this story as another example of God's Divine Intervention. She agreed to let me share the story and agreed to write part of this chapter…

"My name is Barbara, and I would like to share a blessing I received from God. I grew up in a home with four siblings, two older and two younger. Yes, I was the middle child… ugh!

As a middle child I always felt like I did not belong. I wanted to hang with the older siblings, and of course, they did not want this younger sister being part of their group.

Growing up I tried to belong and fit in. I wanted to be part of the crowd. We were raised in a home that was dysfunctional and my mom was very involved in church. My dad did not want anything to do with church. But I am thankful for the teachings and instruction I did get in Sunday school; because of that I gave my life to Jesus as a young child.

As I got into my teenage years my mom turned away from the Lord and decided to live a life that was so different from what I was taught as a child. When my mom walked away from the Lord that created questions in my own life. Was God real?

I made it known to my mom that I thought her actions were inappropriate and because of that I found myself on my own at the age of seventeen. I quit going to church and now at seventeen I felt lost, sad, and confused. I remember eating peanut butter for two weeks because I couldn't afford anything else.

I was searching for love; yes, in all the wrong places. I attended a church service at my old church, and I was yearning for God to bring me out of the hell I was experiencing. On that following Monday I received a call from the pastor, and he said he was coming out to the area where I lived to visit someone in a Boy's Home and asked if he could stop and talk to me. I said, "Sure."

I thought that maybe he was going to come by and give me some words of encouragement and wisdom. He sat and spoke to me briefly and then asked if he could use my restroom. I did not think anything about it. As he came out of the bathroom, he asked me what was in the room that adjoined the restroom; I walked in and that is when he violated me, it was horrific! When he was finished, he got up and looked at me and said that he needed to do that because he was thinking about leaving his wife for another woman in the church!

I was devastated!

I went back to the church the following Sunday and to my amazement, this pastor who just violated me days before was preaching on adultery! I got up in the middle of the service and walked to the back of the church and slammed the door as I left. At that point my faith was destroyed; I was broken and wondered how could this happen to me?

Shortly after that I got involved with my first husband… yes, husband number one. We were together for a total of ten years. We lived together and I had a child out of wedlock. He was abusive, an alcoholic, and a cheater. I stayed in the relationship because I needed someone to love me. To be honest I did not know what love really was. I was young and through those ten years I experienced more heartache than any person should.

He was diagnosed as a bipolar manic-depressive schizophrenic. I experienced some of the most horrifying things during this time. It was very scary when he would lose control and his schizophrenia would take over. He would think he was the antichrist and use the Bible in an ungodly way. He had me consumed with fear! We had a little girl whom I love dearly, and I knew for the sake of our safety we had to get out of the situation. I finally mustered enough nerve to get a divorce and run from that relationship.

Five years later I met my second husband. He was going through a divorce, and we started to date. We dated for five years, then I got pregnant, and we got married. This was another marriage that happened for all the wrong reasons, and it did not last. Six months after our daughter was born he asked me for a divorce. I did not go through the craziness I did with my first husband, but he drank a lot and was a womanizer. I was jealous and did not want the divorce; I just wanted to be loved.

It became apparent that he was involved with another woman. He threatened to take our daughter away from me and I went through nine more years of hell. I prayed and asked God *why*, and I felt that I was being punished. He was Catholic and I had to go to the Catholic Church and go through classes to join. I had completed the classes and was going to be accepted into the church, but the priest called me and said that he had spoken with my ex-husband and felt that I was joining the Catholic Church for all the wrong reasons and that they would not accept me into the church. I told the priest that I did not believe that God would turn me away. This again was devastating, and I was wondering why all these things were happening.

Another five years went by, and I met my third husband. I fell madly in love with him. I really believed he loved me, but having two children from two different marriages, and all the dysfunctional baggage I was carrying made this marriage very shaky. My kids did not care for him and six years into the marriage I found out he also had a drinking problem and was a habitual liar. I decided enough is enough; I left and filed for divorce. I cried many tears and even went back to church. I would continuously pray, "Lord, bring John back to me if it be your will." Well, I guess it was not God's will because he never came back, and I am now sure that it was a good thing.

I then escaped into gambling. I started with just a few dollars a week that grew to hundreds. It was my escape from the hurt and pain. One day I dropped to my knees and asked God to help me out of the mess that was created through all the bad decisions I'd made in the past 45 years. The Lord gave me the strength to sign myself off the casinos in Missouri and Illinois. I felt like a real load had been lifted off my back. It was not easy, but I started to see the light at the end of the tunnel. Not all the heartache was gone, but I know now that God loves me, and He has proven that in so many ways in the past years."

Reading Barb's background will help you understand this Divine Intervention. Sue and I had been praying for Barb's recovery from the open-heart surgery, and for whatever else God knew she needed. We believed her finances were a big concern, so we planned to give her $1000. We did not want to send a check because we also wanted to spend time with her.

September 26, 2021, was the date we set to drive to St. Louis for our visit and to give her the check. That morning before I wrote the check, I felt the Holy Spirit nudging me that it was not enough. Sue and I prayed specifically about this. More than anything we wanted Barb to see that this check was not really coming from us but coming from the Lord and that He was only using us as a tool.

I went to my office, got out the checkbook and was starting to write a check for $1500. However, before I started writing I sensed the Holy Spirit telling me to write the check for $1600. It seemed like an odd amount, but I did not question the figure. We had just finished praying that the Lord would use this in a special way, and I really believed it.

Sue and I enjoy traveling, and the two-hour drive to Barb's house was pleasant. Barb was waiting for us when we arrived, and our plans were to go out together for lunch wherever she wanted to go. Before we left, we spent a few minutes visiting inside her home. While Sue and Barb were in the living room talking, I walked into the kitchen and placed the check on the kitchen counter in an inconspicuous place.

Barb wanted to go to Applebee's and that sounded good to us. We enjoyed our meal, but even better we loved our visit. We spent over two hours talking. I tend to probe people with questions, and she didn't mind. It had been a while since we had shared together, and this was great. Our conversation was mainly about the Lord Jesus and having a relationship with Him, and how much He cares and loves us. We could tell that Barb's heart was being deeply touched.

Towards the end of our two hours, I asked Barb this question, "Does the amount of $1600 have any significant meaning to you?"

She paused for a few moments and then her eyes got wide, and she said, "Yes, it does! That's how much I owe on my medical bill!" I looked straight into her eyes with great compassion and said, "Barb, the Lord Jesus loves you so much and He brought Sue and me to meet with you today and give you something that only He knew you needed. When you go home, look on your kitchen counter and you will see a check for you in the amount of $1600." Her mouth fell open and tears began to well up in her eyes.

We were so excited and amazed to see the Divine Intervention of the Lord with Barbara. The miraculous workings of the Holy Spirit never become a casual experience!

AN AMAZING JOURNEY

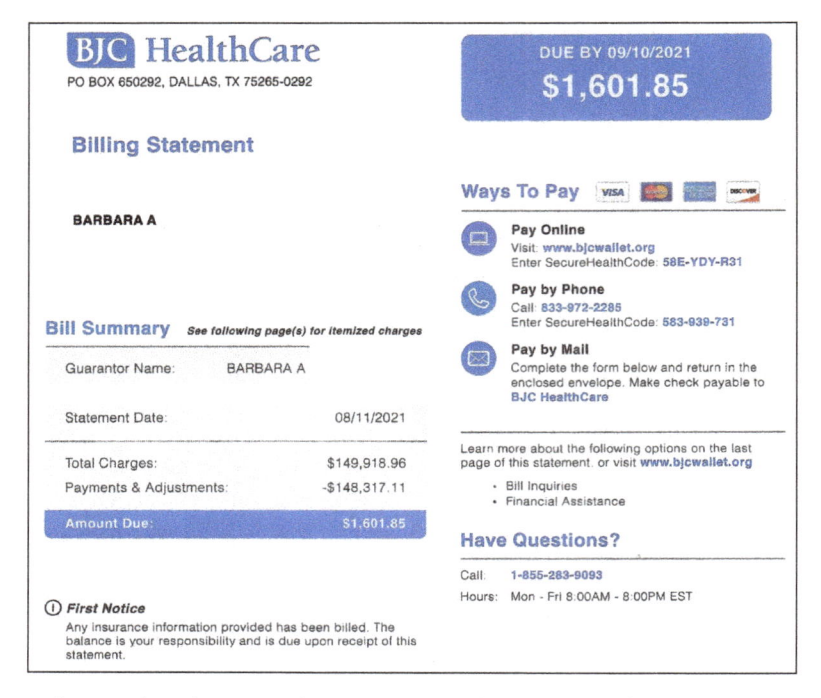

> **BJC HealthCare**
> PO BOX 650292, DALLAS, TX 75265-0292
>
> DUE BY 09/10/2021
> **$1,601.85**
>
> **Billing Statement**
>
> BARBARA A
>
> **Bill Summary** *See following page(s) for itemized charges*
>
> | | |
> |---|---|
> | Guarantor Name: | BARBARA A |
> | Statement Date: | 08/11/2021 |
> | Total Charges: | $149,918.96 |
> | Payments & Adjustments: | -$148,317.11 |
> | **Amount Due:** | **$1,601.85** |
>
> **First Notice**
> Any insurance information provided has been billed. The balance is your responsibility and is due upon receipt of this statement.
>
> **Ways To Pay**
>
> Pay Online — Visit: www.bjcwallet.org — Enter SecureHealthCode: 58E-YDY-R31
>
> Pay by Phone — Call: 833-972-2285 — Enter SecureHealthCode: 583-939-731
>
> Pay by Mail — Complete the form below and return in the enclosed envelope. Make check payable to BJC HealthCare
>
> Learn more about the following options on the last page of this statement, or visit www.bjcwallet.org
> • Bill Inquiries
> • Financial Assistance
>
> **Have Questions?**
> Call: 1-855-263-9093
> Hours: Mon - Fri 8:00AM - 8:00PM EST

The Lord spoke to my heart to write the amount of $1600 on the check. Her exact balance on her medical bill was $1601.85!

Why did God do this? It was very obvious!

All through Barb's story we hear something being repeated many times… "She was needing and wanting to be loved."

The apostle Paul prayed this prayer for the Ephesians…

*"For this reason I kneel before the Father, from whom his whole family in heaven and on earth derives its name. I pray that out of his glorious riches he may strengthen you with power through his Spirit in your inner being, so that Christ may dwell in your hearts through faith. And **I pray that you, being rooted and established in love, may have power, together with all the saints, to grasp how wide and long and high and deep is the love of***

Christ, and to know this love that surpasses knowledge—*that you may be filled to the measure of all the fullness of God" (Eph. 3:14-19 NIV).*

This is exactly what the Lord Jesus was showing Barb. We were only an instrument being used by Him to show His great love for her!

19

Conclusion

It has been my sincere desire to stir up your heart. I pray that this book has been contagious! What has God done in your life that would cause you to build your own memorial of remembrance?

Recently, Sue and I visited with some friends, and we were sharing what I call "God Stories". They got so excited recalling events in their own lives that were stories of God's Divine Intervention. I believe every Christian could and should do the same.

The Bible clearly addresses the disastrous results of forgetting the wonderful things God has done…

*"No sooner had Gideon died than the Israelites again prostituted themselves to the Baals. They set up Baal-Berith as their god and **did not remember the LORD their God, who had rescued them** from the hands of all their enemies on every side"* (Jud. 8:33-34 NIV).

Having a short-term memory of God's blessings and Divine Intervention has been a "spiritual dementia" down through the ages. Is it any surprise?…

"The thief comes only to steal and kill and destroy…" (Jo. 10:10 NIV)

Conclusion

It's very easy for Satan to kill and destroy after he has stolen from your mind the remembrance of God's great deeds!

Nehemiah reminded God's people of their forefathers and what happened to them…

*"But they, our forefathers, became arrogant and stiff-necked, and did not obey your commands. They refused to listen and **failed to remember the miracles** you performed among them"* (Neh. 9:16-17 NIV).

The psalmist also writes about how the loss of memory grieves the Spirit of God and leads to disaster…

*"Again and again, they put God to the test; they vexed the Holy One of Israel. **They did not remember his power**— the day he redeemed them from the oppressor, the day he displayed his miraculous signs in Egypt, his wonders in the region of Zoan"* (Ps. 78:41-43 NIV).

Again, the psalmist writes…

*"When our fathers were in Egypt, they gave no thought to your miracles; **they did not remember** your many kindnesses, and they rebelled by the sea, the Red Sea"* (Ps. 106:7 NIV).

Jesus rebuked his disciples for the lack of remembering the miracle he had done in feeding the multitudes…

*"Do you still not understand? **Don't you remember** the five loaves for the five thousand, and how many basketfuls you gathered? Or the seven loaves for the four thousand, and how many basketfuls you gathered?"* (Mat. 16:9-10 NIV)

In writing this book, it has not been my intention to elevate myself to an exclusive position in hearing God! As we separate our heart from the things of this world, our sensitivity to His voice becomes more discerning.

As of this writing I have been in the ministry nearly forty-seven years. My goal has never been the *size* of my ministry but the *quality of my relationship* with Jesus Christ. When the Bible speaks about us *walking with Jesus Christ*, that is not a suggestion or a theory, but an experience that is life-changing!

In the Old Testament we read a story about a man named Enoch. There is not much said about him, but what we know is fascinating. When he was sixty-five years old, he became the father of Methuselah, who lived to be the oldest man on this earth, 969 years! Then we read these tremendous words about Enoch…

"When Enoch had lived sixty-five years, he became the father of Methuselah. And after he became the father of Methuselah, **Enoch walked with God three hundred years** *and had other sons and daughters. Altogether, Enoch lived three hundred sixty-five years.* **Enoch walked with God; then he was no more, because God took him away"** *(Gen. 5:21-24 NIV).*

The chances of God rapturing you by yourself is unlikely, but the blessing of walking with God is priceless!

I would never try to teach a formula or a method in hearing the voice of God; that would be disastrous. Every story in this book was initiated by God, not by me. It seems like there is always someone trying to come up with a method or a twelve-step program in trying to get God to do what *we want*; I do not suggest that approach.

The prophet Micah, in the Old Testament, addresses this so well. Micah does not deny the desirability of sacrifices but shows that it does no good to offer them without obedience. We are living in a new covenant age, and our relationship is with Jesus Christ, and not by the letter of the law, rituals, and religious sacrifices, but by having a living abiding relationship with the living God through his Son Jesus! Read these words written by the prophet Micah…

Conclusion

"With what shall I come before the LORD and bow down before the exalted God? Shall I come before him with burnt offerings, with calves a year old? Will the LORD be pleased with thousands of rams, with ten thousand rivers of oil? Shall I offer my firstborn for my transgression, the fruit of my body for the sin of my soul? ***He has showed you, O man, what is good. And what does the LORD require of you? To act justly and to love mercy and to walk humbly with your God"*** *(Mic. 6:6 NIV).*

Thank you for taking the time to read this book! Correspondence is encouraged and appreciated, and I can be reached at todd@toddgreiner.com.